C000172285

Before the Law

Before the Law

The Complete Text of *Préjugés*

Jacques Derrida

*Translated by Sandra van Reenen
and Jacques de Ville*

A Univocal Book

University of Minnesota Press

Minneapolis

London

Published by the University of Minnesota Press
111 Third Avenue South, Suite 290
Minneapolis, MN 55401–2520
http://www.upress.umn.edu

Printed in the United States of America on acid-free paper

The University of Minnesota is an equal-opportunity educator and
employer.

23 22 21 20 19 18   10 9 8 7 6 5 4 3 2 1

Library of Congress Cataloging-in-Publication Data
Names: Derrida, Jacques, author. | Van Reenen, Sandra, translator. | De Ville,
Jacques, translator.
Title: Before the law : the complete text of Préjugés / Jacques Derrida;
translated by Sandra van Reenen and Jacques de Ville.
Other titles: Prejuges, devant la loi. English
Description: Minneapolis : University of Minnesota Press, [2018] | Series:
A Univocal book | Proceedings of the 1982 Colloquium in Cerisy-la-
Salle, France. | Includes bibliographical references and index. |
Identifiers: LCCN 2018024546 (print) | ISBN 978-1-5179-0551-4 (pb)
Subjects: LCSH: Judicial process—Congresses. | Judgment—Congresses.
| Law—Methodology—Congresses. | Law—Philosophy—Congresses.
| Law—Interpretation and construction—Congresses. | Procedure (Law)—
Congresses. | Lyotard, Jean-Francois, 1924–1998.
Classification: LCC K213 .D4713 2018 (print) | DDC 340/.1—dc23
LC record available at https://lccn.loc.gov/2018024546

Contents

Translators' Preface

Derrida's text "Préjugés: Before the Law," presented at the 1982 Colloquium at Cerisy, is appearing here for the first time in full in English translation. The colloquium was organized by Michel Enaudeau and Jean-Loup Thébaud, and took place from July 24 to August 3, with the theme Comment juger? (à partir du travail de Jean-François Lyotard). The conference proceedings were published under the title La Faculté de Juger.[1] Translations of this text have thus far appeared in German under the title Préjugés—Vor dem Gesetz and in Japanese, under the title Kafukaron.[2] Only an earlier, shorter presentation by Derrida at the Royal Philosophical Society in London, with the focus on Kafka's "Before the Law," has up to now appeared in English translation.[3] Because of the lack of an English translation, the

---

1. Jacques Derrida et al, *La Faculté de Juger* (Paris: Les Éditions de Minuit, 1985), 87–139.

2. See Jacques Derrida, *Préjugés:Vor dem Gesetz*, ed. Peter Engelmann (Vienna: Passagen Verlag, 1992) and *Kafukaron*, trans. Nobutaka Miura (Tokyo:Asahi syuppansya, 1986).

3. See "Before the Law," trans. Avital Ronell and Christine Roulston, in Jacques Derrida, *Acts of Literature*, ed. Derek Attridge (New York: Routledge, 1992), 181–220; and "Devant la Loi," trans. Avital Ronell, in *Kafka and the Contemporary Critical Performance*, ed. Alan Udoff (Bloomington: Indiana University Press, 1987), 128–49. We benefited greatly from these English translations as well as the German translation.

untranslated part of this text has, since the publication of the French original in 1985, seldom been referred to in academic publications in English.

The importance of "*Préjugés*: Before the Law" for Derrida's oeuvre, and for the question of judgment in general, was recently highlighted by Gasché's analysis of this text in "Have We Done with the Empire of Judgment?"[4] "*Préjugés*: Before the Law" should, as Gasché also contends, be read with other texts of Derrida that touch on the issue of judgment, such as *The Truth in Painting*, "Economimesis," *Glas,* and "Force of Law: The Mystical Foundation of Authority."[5] The present translation of "*Préjugés:* Before the Law," with judgment as its point of departure, now also calls for a rereading of the previously translated part, with its focus on Kafka's "Before the Law," and which deals specifically with the question of the essence of literature, the role of the title, singularity, the law of law, and Freud's reflections on the origin of law in *Totem and Taboo*.[6] This translation furthermore casts light on the relation in Derrida's thinking between judgment and decision, as for example explored in *Politics of Friendship*.[7]

4. See Rodolphe Gasché, *Deconstruction, Its Force, Its Violence: together with "Have We Done with the Empire of Judgment?"* (Albany: State University of New York Press, 2016).

5. See Jacques Derrida, *The Truth in Painting,* trans. Geoff Bennington and Ian McLeod (Chicago: University of Chicago Press, 1987); "Economimesis," in *The Derrida Reader: Writing Performances,* ed. Julian Wolfreys (Lincoln: University of Nebraska Press, 1998), 263–93; *Glas,* trans. John P. Leavey Jr. and Richard Rand (Lincoln: University of Nebraska Press, 1986); and "Force of Law: The Mystical Foundation of Authority," in *Acts of Religion,* ed. Gil Anidjar (New York: Routledge, 2002), 228–98.

6. Sigmund Freud, *Totem and Taboo,* in *The Standard Edition of the Complete Psychological Works of Sigmund Freud,* ed. and trans. James Strachey (London: Vintage, 2001) 13:1–161.

7. Jacques Derrida, *Politics of Friendship,* trans. George Collins (London: Verso, 1997).

The translators would like to thank David Culpin for acting as first reader of the translation.

Jacques de Ville would like to acknowledge the financial support provided by the South African National Research Foundation.

Préjugés
Before the Law

Learning does the same; . . . even our system of
Law, they say, bases the truth of its justice
upon legal fictions.

—Montaigne, *Essays* II.12

How to judge—Jean-François Lyotard?[1]

In the light of a certain number of what, these days, are called pragmatic givens, the situation, the context, the addressees, the sender, especially the scansion of the sentence, its punctuation, if it were to be written down, my question "How-to-judge-Jean-François-Lyotard?" can mean things and have effects that are utterly heterogeneous. The highest probability, but see this only as a probability, is that here and now I am not addressing it directly to Jean-François Lyotard. Unless, depending on the way the apostrophe is shaped, I address it to him, believing him to be here: "How do we judge, Jean-François Lyotard?"

I have already quoted my line of approach [*attaque*], my first sentence, several times ("How to judge—Jean-François Lyotard?"). Why this first sentence? First of all, you will have guessed this already and I will say something more about it shortly, in order to break out, in a friendly way, of that comfort zone into which there is a risk that the new genre practiced by the *Décades*[2] might fall, the

1. [The theme of the conference where Derrida presented this paper asked how judging should take place and was specifically focused on Lyotard's oeuvre: *Comment juger? (à partir du travail de Jean-François Lyotard)*.—Trans.]

2. [See further Jacques Derrida, *Rogues: Two Essays on Reason*, trans. Pascale-Anne Brault and Michael Naas (Stanford, Calif.: Stanford University Press, 2005), 2.—Trans.]

new genre that, for a thousand good reasons of which I
previously approved and which remain valid, a genre that
might claim to unfold "beginning with—" or, better still,
"beginning with the work of—"³ rather than speaking directly about—or addressing itself directly to—someone. In
that, there is denegation and avoidance. Whatever its legit-
imacy (politeness, discretion on both sides, work rather
than celebration, etc.), my opening question should not be
ignored. Also, I have quoted my first sentence to immediately indebt us to another quotation, taken from *The Postmodern Condition,* and to this passage in particular:

> It cannot be denied that there is persuasive force
> in the idea that context control and domination are
> inherently better than their absence. The performa-
> tivity criterion has its "advantages." It excludes in
> principle adherence to a metaphysical discourse; it
> requires the renunciation of fables; it demands clear
> minds and cold wills; it replaces *the definition of
> essences with the calculation of interactions* [em-
> phasis added, J.D.]; it makes the "players" assume re-
> sponsibility not only for the statements they propose,
> but also for the rules to which they submit those
> statements in order to render them acceptable. It
> brings the pragmatic functions of knowledge clearly
> to light, to the extent that they seem to relate to the
> criterion of efficiency: the pragmatics of argumenta-
> tion, of the production of proof, of the transmission
> of learning, and of the apprenticeship of the imag-
> ination. It also contributes to elevating all language
> games to self-knowledge, even those not within the

---

3. [See, for example, the conference at Cerisy held from July 23
to August 2, 1980, organized by Philippe Lacoue-Labarthe and Jean-
Luc Nancy with the theme *Les fins de l'homme (à partir du travail
de Jacques Derrida).*—Trans.]

realm of canonical knowledge. It tends to jolt everyday discourse into a kind of metadiscourse: ordinary statements are now displaying a propensity *for self-citation* [emphasis added, J.D.], and the various pragmatic posts are tending to make an indirect connection even to current messages concerning them.[4]

Given that the question has been asked, and quoted, and given that the person it concerns has already been quoted, "How to judge Jean-François Lyotard?", do I have the right to turn this question into another one: "Who is Jean-François Lyotard?" Would I, by answering one of these questions, have answered the other? In the way I have expressed it (Who is Jean-François Lyotard), no trick of punctuation or intonation can make of it a question addressed to him, but only to a third party sitting in judgment, unless, knowing him to be here, I play subtly with the proper name and with the strange relationship between a proper name and the person who bears it in order to ask him directly, not "who are you" but "who is Jean-François Lyotard?", and by doing so I would be referring not just to the name itself but to the bearer of the name. It seems as though he is here but, if I tried to demonstrate that, by saying it or by naming him, I would quickly become entangled in deictic paradoxes. I would have to ask him, as the expert, for help and make an interminable detour by way of *Discourse, Figure*.[5] The passage on *Dialectic and deictic*—which is also a particular interpretation of sense-certainty in the *Phenomenology of Spirit*—proposes the

---

4. [Jean-François Lyotard, *The Postmodern Condition: A Report on Knowledge,* trans. Geoff Bennington and Brian Massumi (Manchester: Manchester University Press, 1979), 62—Trans.]

5. [Jean-François Lyotard, *Discourse, Figure,* trans. Antony Hudeck and Mary Lydon (Minneapolis: University of Minnesota Press, 2011. Subsequent page citations are in the text.—Trans.]

word "dia-deictics" [*"dia-déictique"*] to indicate a "sort of mute, gestural 'discourse,'" and repeatedly mentions the word "here" (35). But, if I have understood him correctly, Lyotard specifies a little further on, and in opposition to Hegelian mediation, that "dia-deictics can be a type of dialectics, but it is not a discourse" (38). And the situation becomes much more complicated when a gesture that is used to point out is accompanied by the enunciation of a proper name, since this enunciation can be concealed beneath a huge variety of modes and masks, among which is the one that we name the call, or the apostrophe.

Those among you who are biased [*prévenus*][6] will already have understood the title *Préjugés*.[7] And that is because they are *prévenus,* and whoever uses this word—*prévenus*—is already moving in that zone of language where the legal code, the code [*du code*],[8] the judicial code, even the penal code cuts across all other codes. For in French the term *prévenu* is also applied to someone who has been taken in for questioning before the

---

6. [The French *prévenus* poses similar difficulties of translation as the title *Préjugés* (see note 7). The adjective *prévenu, prévenue* is formed by the past participle of the verb *prévenir,* which inter alia means "to inform, to warn, to tell," as well as "to predispose (somebody toward)" or "to prejudice (somebody against)." As adjective, *prévenu* can bear the meaning of (being) "biased," as well as having been "charged" or "accused (of a crime)." See further in the text above Derrida's explication of this word.—Trans.]

7. [As appears from Derrida's analysis, this part of the title can bear a variety of meanings and is strictly speaking untranslatable, which is why it has been left untranslated in the title of the present text. The title is an important "theme" in many of Derrida's texts, including *Given Time: 1. Counterfeit Money,* trans. Peggy Kamuf (Chicago: The University of Chicago Press, 1992), 82–98; *Dissemination,* trans. Barbara Johnson (London: Continuum, 2004), 192–95; and *Parages,* trans. Tom Conley et al. (Stanford, Calif.: Stanford University Press, 2011), 193–215.—Trans.]

8. [This may be a reference to the French civil code—Trans.]

indictment or the judgment.[9] The state of being-questioned [*L'être-prévenu*] is therefore a category-specific category. It is defined by its relationship to the *kategorein,* that is to say, accusation, blame, the act of denunciation as much as enunciation, of saying, attributing, judging, and making known.[10] When I say "How to judge Jean-François Lyotard?" or "Who is Jean-François Lyotard?" I am being categorical, I am calling for a categorical reply, implicating him in a scene of preliminary enquiry toward which various movements of denunciation would be rushing, if they had not done so already, ready to speak in order to save or betray, to reveal or expose, to accuse or plead, to defend or bear witness, to renounce or denounce until the enquiry takes place, even if the case is dismissed. But when a case is

---

9. [This appears to be an allusion to the procedure followed in terms of the French Criminal Procedure Code by an investigating judge *(juge d'instruction)* who may "place under judicial examination only those persons against whom there is strong and concordant evidence making it probable that they may have participated, as perpetrator or accomplice, in the commission of the offences he is investigating" (art 80–81), http://www.legislationline.org/documents/section/criminal-codes/country/30 (accessed May 30, 2017).—Trans.]

10. [See *Online Etymology Dictionary,* entry "category": "1580s, from Middle French *catégorie,* from Late Latin *categoria,* from Greek *kategoria* 'accusation, prediction, category,' verbal noun from *kategorein* 'to speak against; to accuse, assert, predicate,' from *kata* 'down to' (or perhaps 'against;' . . .) + *agoreuein* 'to harangue, to declaim (in the assembly),' from *agora* 'public assembly'. . . . Original sense of 'accuse' weakened to 'assert, name' by the time Aristotle applied *kategoria* to his 10 classes of things that can be named," , http://www.etymonline.com/ (accessed May 30, 2017); see further Jacques Derrida, *The Death Penalty,* vol. 1, trans. Peggy Kamuf (Chicago: The University of Chicago Press, 2014), 5, where *katēgoria* is understood as accusation, charge. In the present text, Derrida also points to the *pré-* in *préjugés,* which alludes to the precategorical or the not-yet-categorical, that is, to the pre-origin of judgment.—Trans.]

dismissed this is still a legal event, it is, in terms of the law, a juridical decision, a judgment of nonjudgment.

Those who are here *prévenus*—beginning with Lyotard who, more than anyone else, is summoned to appear—will have quickly understood that under the title *Préjugés,* and in accordance with a tendency that I rarely resist, I am preparing to speak (and this is to be feared) only about the title, that is to say, *Préjugés.* The referential function of a title is very paradoxical. We shall see that these paradoxes are always juridico-topological. Because of the place that it occupies and the context to which it gives a structure, a title is both the proper name of the discourse or the work to which it gives a title, and the name of the subject that the work discusses or about which it speaks. The nature of this reference, which is at least bifid, would of itself justify an avid rereading of *Discourse, Figure* at its most disturbing, active, and boisterous center.

Those among you who are *prévenus* will also have understood: in this normally separated, cut off, insular place that one must always give to a title, whilst also surrounding it with a certain contextual blank space, its meaning suspended by an *epoché,* in a sentence or a nonsentence that some people would call abnormal (is *Préjugés* a sentence?), the word *préjugés* holds the grammatical potential of the attribute and the noun in reserve. The word can be an adjective and a noun, but for the moment it is neither one nor the other. This means that, before we are allowed to judge or decide, the two categories of being and having are suspended in its *epoché.* As a noun it refers to the prejudices that some or others of us could *have* or that we might possibly entertain on the subject of judgment and on the question of knowing "how to judge." As an attribute (which is a rarer usage, and slightly forced, though grammatically possible in an unfinished sentence and as allowed here by the play[11] of the title) the title would refer to the prejudged beings [*les êtres préjugés*] that we *are*. It would be gesturing toward those who, before the law [*devant la loi*], find themselves to be prejudged [*préjugés*]. Not toward the prejudices that we have, but toward those that we are or that we make of each other. Or even toward the prejudged [*préjugés*] that we are, though this has been caused by no one else. For it is possible to be judged, or to have been judged, or to be judged in advance, even though no one is there or has ever been there—and that is what I will speak to you about—to have judged us or to have had the right to judge us.

This title is therefore untranslatable. It belongs to the play of transformation inherent in the French language; it is bound by the law of that language and derives from it all its powers; it also draws the effects of its anomaly from a French linguistic normality or normativity. In the case of *Vorurteil* or *prejudice*,*[12] the entire economy of this play would have to be abandoned and, in the best case, others would have to be invented, others that were very different. I shall return to the law of this relationship between law and language.

But in this title, as in all titles, the adjectival or attributive function of the word *préjugés* is nevertheless inscribed within a wider, nominative function. For any title is, according to the law [*en droit*], the name of the text or the work to which it is given, even though it is also an original part of it; and from a place that is prescribed for it by a legal

---

11. [The notion of "play" *(jeu)* is specifically explored by Derrida in, for example, *Of Grammatology,* trans. Gayatri Chakravorty Spivak (Baltimore: The John Hopkins University Press, 1976), 50, and *Writing and Difference,* trans. Alan Bass (Chicago: The University of Chicago Press, 1978), 279. Derrida in these texts contrasts two forms of "play": (1) play based on a fundamental ground, coupled with security, in the sense of an origin, a full presence; and (2) play without any security, placing oneself completely at risk.—Trans.]

12. [Words followed by an asterisk are in English in the original. —Trans.]

code [*droit codé*], the title name must also show and indicate, if at all possible, that which it names. It is about this that I will speak to you, about this double (at least double) referential function of a title that belongs structurally to that class of *dissoi logoi* known to sophistry. Lyotard gives remarkable examples of this in *Duchamp's TRANS/formers*,[13] and these are precisely examples belonging to the categorical domains of accusation, praise, and blame. But, since I am going to spend my time, and yours, playing with and transforming the prejudices [*les préjugés*] of my title, you should also know, when I cite *Les transformateurs Duchamp / Duchamp's TRANS/formers,* that everything I am striving to invent[14] during these four or five hours is only a marginal, oblique and dubious, para-deictic (that is to say mute [*muette*])[15] interpretation of items 7, 8, 9, and 10 of the chapter entitled *The Glass,* that is to say, *Title of the* Glass, *the narrative* (149),[16] *Title of the* Glass, *the logical* (151), *Title of the* Glass, *the paradoxical* (153), and *Title of the* Glass, *hinge* (153). Those who do not believe me will be able to check. After a certain point I will no longer use the word *préjugés,* but I will continue to make it undergo a series of almost imperceptible transformations that will become the title, or at least a part of the title, of my speech. With reference to *Large Glass,* Lyotard

13. [Jean-François Lyotard, *Les transformateurs Duchamp / Duchamp's TRANS/formers,* trans. Ian McLeod (Leuven: Leuven University Press, 2010), 82–85.—Trans.]

14. [On invention, see further Jacques Derrida, *Psyche: Inventions of the Other,* vol. 1,, ed. Peggy Kamuf and Elizabeth Rottenberg (Stanford, Calif.: Stanford University Press, 2007), 1–47.—Trans.]

15. [The French *muette* can also be translated as "dumb," yet because of the latter's ambiguity, we opted here for "mute." Although Derrida is indeed speaking here, he will say nothing explicitly concerning the interpretation of these items in *Duchamp's TRANS/formers.*—Trans.]

16. [Here and following, Derrida is citing pages of Lyotard, *Les transformateurs Duchamp.*—Trans.]

quotes Duchamp:"I was always going to give an important role to the title which I added and which I treated as an invisible color" (153), and then makes wonderful use of the paradoxical logic in this treatment of the title, this "tautology, or paradox of class of all classes" (153), which derives from the fact that, "[i]f the title can act as a color, it is because a color acts as a name (of a color). Inasmuch as it is colored, the picture is a statement, at least a combination of names denuded of meanings, in a word: a title. The title of the *Glass* is a color, it is the work, or a part of the work. And the colors of the work act as its title. Thus the title is doubly paradoxical . . ." (153).

So I continue, but not without mentioning at this point the transformation, or the transformations of the title *Préjugés.* The marker of the plural in the title, the *s* at the end of *Préjugés,* indicates the proliferating play of these trans-deformations. I will be very careful not to attempt to explicate the context we are here dealing with. A complete explication of it is, by the very nature of things, impossible, not least because any such explication should itself be taken into account [*devrait s'y compter*]. But, although we know very little, what we do know is enough to understand that the word *préjugés* is here not merely pointing in the direction of something that is judged in advance or that has already been judged, a pre-reflexive decision or a received opinion. The para-normality of the quasi-sentence that constitutes the title means that the noun *Préjugés* can also name something that is *not yet* either a category or a predicate. And the *not-yet* of the pre-predicative or the pre-categorical can also be divided into two parts. It is everything that Ponge says about *pré* that we should read here.[17]

---

17. [See Francis Ponge, *The Making of the Pré,* trans. Lee Fahnestock (Columbia: University of Missouri Press, 1979), and for commentary, Jacques Derrida, *Signéponge/Signsponge,* trans. Richard Rand (New York: Columbia University Press, 1984).—Trans.]

The *pre-* of pre-judgment can be homogenous with what it precedes, prepares, or anticipates, a sort of judgment before the judgment, which can in its turn be either simply hidden, enveloped, reserved, or (and this would be entirely different) denied: not the denial that is a singular form of judgment, but a denial of judgment itself. And you know that, among other possible readings, this text by Lyotard, his most continuous, could be understood as a vigilant and merciless meditation on the effects of denial.[18] This meditation complicates and progressively extends, right up to the most recent studies (up to what could be called a pragmatic paradoxology or a paradoxical pragmatology) the initial statement of this problematic, which was already complex, in the ideas of Freud, Benveniste, Hyppolite, and Lacan. As you know, Lyotard retranslated *Die Verneinung*[19] in *Discourse, Figure,* and this is not without significance. But, having thus interpreted it, he never stopped retranslating, transforming, and deforming Freud's interrogation of judgment and of the "logical scandal that arises in the analytic interpretation. 'It is *not* my mother,' says the analysand. 'We amend this to: it is therefore his mother,' says Freud."[20]

So, the *pré-* of *préjugés* can be homogenous with the order of judgment in these two very different modes, either implicit presupposition or denial, which can itself be put forward either as a categorical denial or as a denial *of the* categorical. But the *pré-* of *préjugés* can also remain

---

18. [See further Jacques Derrida, *Psyche: Inventions of the Other,* vol. 2, ed. Peggy Kamuf and Elizabeth Rottenberg (Stanford, Calif.: Stanford University Press, 2008), 143–95—Trans.]

19. [See Sigmund Freud, "Negation," in *The Standard Edition of the Complete Psychological Works of Sigmund Freud,* ed. and trans. James Strachey (London: Vintage, 2001) 19:233-39.—Trans.]

20. [Lyotard, *Discourse, Figure,* 115; see further Freud, "Negation," 235.—Trans.]

absolutely heterogeneous with the order of all possible judgment, not only *older* (always older) than the judgment that is its origin, but (if it were possible) without any relationship to judicative authority [*l'instance judicative*] in general, to that attitude, operation, and enunciation that is involved in judging.

But what is it that we call judging?

In its very form, the question "How to judge?" seems at least to prejudge [*préjuger*] what it means to judge. The situation is that, since we know, or we *presuppose* what it means to judge, we ask ourselves only *how should we judge?* But, as a title that hangs in suspense, the question "How to judge?" can have a paradoxical effect, a truly paradoxical effect, if a paradox always undermines the certainty of a *doxa,* of an opinion or an accepted judgment, and (here) of a judgment about judgment, of a *préjugé* about judgment, not only as regards what it means to judge, but also as regards the authority of the *ousia* [being], of the *quod* [why], or the *quid* [what], or of the "this is it" with regard to the nature of judgment. In fact, as a title and as a result of its indeterminate, suspended context, "How to judge?" can have a radically critical effect on the logic of the presupposition according to which we must know what it means to judge before asking the question "How to judge?" To begin with the question "How?" and not the question "What is?" can imply that we suspend the classical *prerogative* of judgment, an ontological prerogative requiring that one first say or think the being [*qu'on dise ou pense d'abord l'être*], that one first of all *affirm* the essence, for example, of a function, before asking oneself *how* it functions. This ontological prerogative—which is perhaps not the entire ontology—is pre-judicative in the sense that it implies a pre-judgment [*pré-jugé*] that says that, the essence of judgment being to name the essence (S is P), that very essence of judgment itself is accessible

13

only to a judgment that says S is P before any modalization takes place. It is also a prerogative that the theoretical and the constative have over the performative or the pragmatic, and this prerogative prejudges [*préjuge*], predetermines, or predestines the very essence of judgment and, we could even say, the essence of essence, by submitting it to the question "What is?" It is the confidence of this *préjugé* about judgment and about any pre-judgment that could be upset by a question beginning "How to judge?" Because this question calls into question the entire theoretical-ontological structure that decides in advance [*préjuge*] that one must be able to make a judgment about what judgment *is* before deciding on the *way* in which judgment should be made, etc.

And then, above all, in the reserved force [*la force réservée*] of its own suspension, completely abandoned to the pragmatics of intonation, the question "How to judge?" also implicitly gives expression to the powerlessness, the anxiety, the dread, or the retreat of the person who recuses him- or herself when faced with the undecidable or the *double bind:* how then to judge if one cannot or one must not or one has neither the means nor the right thereto? Or if one has the duty but not the right? How can judgment be made if one cannot *not* judge and yet one has neither the right, nor the power, nor the means? Nor the criteria. That, as you know, is what is required of the just man [*au juste*][21] in *Au juste.*[22] And you know the just man's reply, which is not at all the reply given by the Savoyard Vicar who, at the beginning of his profession of faith, asks: "But who am I? What right have I to judge things, and what

---

21. [The French *au juste* can also mean "exactly".—Trans.]

22. [This is a reference to Jean-François Lyotard and Jean-Loup Thébaud, *Just Gaming,* trans. Samuel Weber (Minneapolis: University of Minnesota Press, 2008). The French title is *Au Juste: Conversations.*—Trans.]

determines my judgments?"[23] and then finds answers to these questions and also criteria for his judgments. The answer to the question put to the just man is: "we judge without criteria. We are in the position of Aristotle's prudent individual, who makes judgments about the just and the unjust without the least criterion . . ." or again: "Absolutely, I judge. But if I am asked by what criteria do I judge, I will have no answer to give . . ."[24] I do not know if the just man is sufficiently prudent when he pretends, in that respect, to identify himself with Aristotle's prudent individual. We shall not ask what his criteria are. But here I interpret the absence of a criterion less as the absence of rules that are determined or determining (that is to say, which are reflective), than as the terrifying or exalting effect of that scene of judgment of which we have just caught a glimpse: since one cannot (without already being subject to prejudice) begin with the question "What is judgment?" since one must begin, without knowing, without assurance, without prejudice, with the question "How to judge?" the absence of a criterion is, one might say, the law. If the criteria were simply available, if the law was present, there, in front of us, there would be no judgment. At best there would be knowledge, technique, application of a code, appearance of a decision, mock trial, or even a narrative [*récit*],[25] a narrative simulacrum on the subject of judgment. There would be no reason to judge or to be anxious about judgment, one would no longer ask oneself "How to judge?"

It is on the subject of this situation that I will tell you my story.

---

23. [See in this regard Jean-Jacques Rousseau, *Emile, or On Education,* trans. Allan Bloom (London: Penguin, 1979), 270. —Trans.]

24. [Lyotard and Thébaud, *Just Gaming,* 14, 15.—Trans.]

25. [See Derrida, *Parages,* 103–91 and 217–49, on the *récit.* At stake here can be said to be a narrative without beginning or end, without content, and without border, in short, a narrative without narrative.—Trans.]

How should Jean-François Lyotard be judged?

Evidently: in this situation where what is happening is that judgment must dispense with criteria and law must dispense with law, in this situation of law being outside-the-law [*hors-la-loi de la loi*] we are all the more required to answer before the law. The absence of criteriology, the unpresentable structure of the law of laws does not obviate the necessity for us to judge in every sense, theoretical and pragmatic, and we have just seen why; on the contrary, that very absence enjoins us to present ourselves before the law and to answer for ourselves *a priori* before the law that is not present [*devant elle qui n'est pas là*].[26] In that sense also *we are,* whatever *préjugés* we may have, *préjugés*. Whatever *préjugés* we may have, that is fundamentally what we are. I will not explore this theme, as one could or should, with reference to Nietzsche or the primordial *Schuldigsein* of which Heidegger speaks and the *Unheimlichkeit* that dwells there [*qui l'habite*], if one might so express it.[27]

Before beginning I must tell you a little of what I will not tell you. Having, after a somewhat confused deliberation, given up the idea of advancing in this or that direction, I judged that I should not give up so completely as to give no idea of what it was that I was giving up. And that, in line with the device of irony, hypocrisy, or denial that is at work in any utterance, I should, in doing so, allow what I said I would not say to declare itself. I have therefore set aside three hypotheses, or three subjects, since that is

---

26. [The French *la loi* (the law) is a feminine noun, taking the subject pronoun *elle,* which can be translated both as "it" and as "she." Pronouns relating to the law will be translated here by employing the neuter "it," yet this "it" should also be heard as "she." —Trans.]

27. [Martin Heidegger, *Being and Time,* trans. John Macquarrie and Edward Robinson (New York: HarperCollins, 1962), 325–35 (section 58). —Trans.]

almost the same word. Here are the three subjects about which, in particular, I will not speak.

The first hypothesis—I would say the first prejudice [*préjugé*] if I had not decided not to utter this word again—is myself. For a few moments I felt the desire to present myself, to appear once more before you who, here, are the law or the guardians of the law [*gardiens de la loi*].[28] To present myself to you as a man alone before the law, not in order to tell you or to ask you who I am, to provoke a judgment by telling a story, but rather to explain myself, with Lyotard of course, on the subject of my relationship with judgment in general. For more than a year, in preparing myself for this session, I have become conscious of the persistent obstinacy with which I have always kept at a distance the theme (yes, I say the theme) of judgment. At bottom, the whole discourse on *différance,* on undecidability, etc., can also be considered as a means of keeping one's distance from judgment in all its forms (predicative, prescriptive; always decisive). It would be easy to show that, beneath this apparent reserve, a judgment is present or has returned, dominating the scene from which it appears to be absent with a tyrannical denial that is all the more stubborn. Nevertheless, in its very appearance, this manifestation (in which I have taken part, and of which I have had my part), which consisted in treating the question of judgment as though it were no longer relevant, that is to say unpresentable, this question may still be considered as significant. Not only in respect of this or that trial

---

28. [The French *gardien* can be translated inter alia as "guard," "warder," "warden," "attendant," "keeper," "caretaker," "guardian," "watchman," and "custodian." Except in cases of direct quotation (where it is translated as "doorkeeper"), it will be rendered here as "guardian." Because of the importance of the notion of guarding in the present text, we have translated the French *garder* in general as "to guard" even though it also bears meanings such as "to keep" or "to retain".—Trans.]

(if one may put it that way) of judgment itself, or at least of the investigation of judgment that was undertaken, but in respect of the epoch [*l'époque*]. And it was an epoch marked: (1) by a phenomenology (it was one of the first interests that I shared with Lyotard, whom I first read as a reader of Husserl, and whom I heard for the first time around 1963 giving a lecture at the Collège Philosophique on time, genetic constitution, *hylè*,[29] etc.), that is to say: *epoché* as suspending the thesis of existence that often, if not always, takes the form of judgment; the de-sedimentation of the predicative layer of experience, the genealogy of judgment following the return to the ante-predicative stratum of perception;[30] (2) by a Heideggerian meditation that passes through a truth that is withdrawn from its judicative form [*forme judicative*]; truth as *adaequatio* is, in its very nature, tied to judgment, to the assertion [*proposition*], that is to say it is *founded on* disclosure that is non-judicative, pre-judicative, another truth. *Aléthéia* is not linked to judgment. This is clearly stated as early as *Sein und Zeit* ("The Concept of the Logos");[31] (3) by a psychoanalytic shake-up, particularly in relation to *Verneinung* [negation], which was undermining any possible assurance provided by a nonparadoxical interpretation of discourse that judges.

One might therefore believe, if that was an epochal moment, an epoch for judgment, that we had done with the reign of judgment that, in fact, constituted the whole of philosophy. Now, the most obvious singularity of Jean-François Lyotard today, the paradox of his signature, is to have inhabited every corner of that epoch and yet to

---

29. [See further Derrida, *Writing and Difference*, 162–64.—Trans.]

30. [See, for example, *The Essential Husserl: Basic Writings in Transcendental Phenomenology*, ed. Donn Welton (Bloomington: Indiana University Press, 1999), 63–65.—Trans.]

31. [See Heidegger, *Being and Time*, 55–58.—Trans.]

have abandoned it; and, from a place that was his alone, to have launched against the epoch, I will not say simply a powerful accusation, but a categorical challenge that I also take to be his laughter. He says to us: you are not done with it, we will never be done with judgment. Your epoch, which is also a *crisis*—and your *epoché* (Husserlian or Heideggerian)—still retains something of an enormous prejudgment in the form of a paradoxical denial in respect of judgment itself. All of that should be looked at again, by bringing into play an alternative (non-Lacanian) psycho-analysis of denial, narrative, paradox, a new pragmatic. Etc.

In effect Lyotard is perhaps someone who also came to tell us something essential—here it would be better to say something decisive, *decisiveness* itself [le décisif *même*]—in the epoch, regarding the epoch, that is, return-ing to the very basis of judgment [*pour ce qui revient à fonder le jugement*]. To put that more simply, we inhab-ited an epoch the *fundamental* formulation of which could be the following: whether founded or not founded, it comes to the same thing, judgment is secondary, the cat-egorical authority is dependent. Some people were say-ing: judgment *is founded,* meaning founded in something other than itself (ante-predictive experience, *aléthéia* as prepropositional disclosure, etc.). Other people were say-ing the opposite, which comes to the same thing: judg-ment is *not founded,* meaning not founded in itself, and therefore illegitimate by its very self and without its own criteria. In both cases, founded or not founded, it was pos-sible to say that judgment is secondary or *inessential:* this is not a decisive philosophical theme, recourse is re-quired to another authority. But, in our epoch, this scene, this scene taken from *modernity* that believes it has done with the classical epoch of judgment, the epoch when the philosophy of judgment (from Plato to Hegel) held sway, Jean-François Lyotard in effect says to us: look out, let me stop you there, there is a paradox, and this is the signature

19

of the postmodern, judgment in fact does not found and is not founded, it is perhaps secondary but it is for that very reason that there is absolutely no question of doing away with it; and, if you think you can do away with it, it will nevertheless not leave you in peace anytime soon. You are pre-judged [*pré-jugés*] by it and, in relation to it, you inhabit pre-judgment [*dans le pré-jugé*]. It is because judgment rests on nothing, does not present itself, and especially not with its philosophical titles, its criteria, and its reason, that is to say its identity card, that (paradoxically) judgment is ineluctable. That is perhaps what Lyotard is saying in this harangue, like a pagan preacher or a sophist who knows neither the law nor the prophets because he knows them too well. He calls us back ceaselessly to a judgment that, although it is not founded, although therefore it is neither the first nor the last, is nonetheless *in progress,* speaking in us before we speak, permanent like a court that is continuously in session and that would be sitting even when no one is present.

And so, when I became aware of this trial I gave up the idea of speaking about myself, because I would have found myself accused along with the whole epoch, and would have wanted to defend myself. I said to myself: It is better to go immediately over to the other side and speak—this was my second hypothesis—not about myself, but about "Lyotard-and-I," about everything that can happen in approximately twenty years, things that I cannot even name, for I find words so inadequate in this context, a common story, a relation without relation between two people, in which one is never sure that they are speaking to each other, that they know each other, that they really read each other, write to each other, address each other directly or indirectly, obliquely accord each other virtual attention that is intense or infinitesimal, sharp and fatally distracted, that misunderstands because of the very strength of its appropriation, and that they forget or do not forget that the other is in the vicinity watching for anything that moves. This is what one should always speak about, you know that it is the essential but that it can be read only between the lines, that it is a text that is mad in its complexity—and I say mad because we are dealing with madness, a *categorical* madness, for each minuscule moment of this madness is certainly infinitely divisible, but within it one would always find judgment. We would never be done with judgment, or rather with that which makes us ask "How to judge." And that is what I hear myself saying via Jean-François Lyotard. So I gave up in advance the idea of speaking about "Lyotard-and-I," but I know that if, one day, this took the form of a narrative about bygone days, there would at least be a chapter entitled "Husserl," another entitled "Levinas," and certainly another entitled "Cerisy." It would go back to at least 1972.[32] As you would almost all be, at one and the same time, both witnesses and actors, judges and the parties involved, I told myself that this was not the time or place to launch into something so serious and so dangerous. I therefore gave in to fear and told myself—the third subject—that the subject of judgment had to be Lyotard. The question "How to judge?" is his; and so to both respect and to break our shared contract, I will begin from Lyotard's work, in the ways that it provokes us and stirs us to think, only on condition that this point of departure will not be an avoidance strategy with respect to the question: Who is Jean-François Lyotard? How to judge him?

At that point I had put myself in the situation of being unable, any longer, to avoid my subject, the third subject, which was also the first, the one guarding something of the other [*l'un gardant de l'autre*], and the one being more untenable and more inevitable than the other. I think that

---

32. [This appears to be a reference to the 1972 Cerisy conference on Nietzsche where both Derrida and Lyotard presented papers. —Trans.]

I have, finally, avoided it, but I am still not sure. In any case, my first challenge, paradoxical but classic, consisted in asking myself if I was going to treat my subject categorically, that is to say in terms of judgment and in terms of generalities (which is just another way of avoiding it), or idiomatically, trying to find some law that would apply only to him, Jean-François Lyotard. Does that exist, a law or a category that applies in only one case [*pour un seul*]?

To whom could I put this question, other than to Jean-François Lyotard himself, in a sort of cry for help, asking him to make that singular law accessible to me or, first of all, to make himself accessible to me, at my request?

I felt I had received a murmured or coded reply from him, in all those places where he talks about the narrative [*narratique*] and about narrative pragmatics, particularly in "Lessons in Paganism,"[33] to which I refer you if you do not know it by heart already.

And so it is in his name, in the name of his narrative pragmatics that I took the decision to allow myself to retell the story that Kafka (as we know) entitled "Vor dem Gesetz." In allowing myself to tell this story in my own way (which I have been doing for almost an hour already, though you would only be able to notice this subsequently), I am perhaps going to postpone judgment once more on the subject of Jean-François Lyotard, who knows? In any event my first line of approach, which might be interpreted as an avoidance, will be to ask myself: what is this text? How to judge it? Is it really a narrative, yes or no? Is it really literature, yes or no? And above all, before all and after all, where do we situate Jean-François Lyotard? Is his place as an actant (the man from the country, the guardian, all the guardians that he imagines behind him)? Is his place that of the

33. [See Jean-François Lyotard, "Lessons in Paganism," trans. David Macey, in *The Lyotard Reader,* ed. Andrew Benjamin (Oxford: Blackwell Publishers, 1998), 122–54.—Trans.]

law, though we do not know if law is or is not an actant in the narrative? Or perhaps it is the place of the title itself that, as we shall see, is larger than the text and larger even than his signature.

We read:

BEFORE THE LAW

BEFORE THE LAW stands a doorkeeper. To this doorkeeper there comes a man from the country and prays for admittance to the Law. But the doorkeeper says that he cannot grant admittance at the moment. The man thinks it over and then asks if he will be allowed in later. "It is possible," says the doorkeeper, "but not at the moment." Since the gate stands open, as usual, and the doorkeeper steps to one side, the man stoops to peer through the gateway into the interior. Observing that, the doorkeeper laughs and says: "If you are so drawn to it, just try to go in despite my veto. But take note: I am powerful. And I am only the least of the doorkeepers. From hall to hall there is one doorkeeper after another, each more powerful than the last. The third doorkeeper is already so terrible that even I cannot bear to look at him." These are difficulties the man from the country has not expected. The Law, he thinks, should surely be accessible at all times and to everyone, but as he now takes a closer look at the doorkeeper in his fur coat, with his big sharp nose and long, thin, black Tartar beard, he decides that it is better to wait until he gets permission to enter. The doorkeeper gives him a stool and lets him sit down at one side of the door. There he sits for days and years. He makes many attempts to be admitted, and wearies the doorkeeper by his importunity. The doorkeeper frequently has little interviews with him, asking him questions about his home and many other things, but the questions are put indifferently, as great lords put them, and always finish with the statement that he cannot be let in yet. The man, who has furnished himself with many things for his journey, sacrifices all he has, however valuable, to bribe the doorkeeper. The doorkeeper accepts everything, but always with the remark: "I am only taking it to keep you from thinking you have omitted anything." During these many years the man fixes his attention almost continuously on the doorkeeper. He forgets the other doorkeepers, and this first one seems to him the sole obstacle preventing access to the Law. He curses his bad luck, in his early years boldly and loudly; later, as he grows old, he only grumbles to himself. He becomes childish, and since in his yearlong [*jahrelangen,* i.e. long lasting or lasting for years (trans.)] contemplation of the doorkeeper he has come to know even the fleas in his fur collar, he begs the fleas as well to help him and to change the doorkeeper's mind. At length his eyesight begins to fail, and he does not know whether the world is really darker or whether his eyes are only deceiving him. Yet in his darkness he is now aware of a radiance that streams inextinguishably from the gateway of the Law. Now he has not very long to live. Before he dies, all his experiences in these long years gather themselves in his head to one point, a question he has not yet asked the doorkeeper. He waves him nearer, since he can no longer raise his stiffening body. The doorkeeper has to bend low toward him, for the difference in height between them has altered much to the man's disadvantage. "What do you want to know now?" asks the doorkeeper; "you are insatiable." "Everyone strives to reach the Law," says the man, "so how does it happen that for all these many years no one but myself has ever begged for

24

admittance?" The doorkeeper recognizes that the man has reached his end, and, to let his failing senses catch the words, roars in his ear: "No one else could ever be admitted here, since this gate was made only for you. I am now going to shut it."

FRANZ KAFKA[34]

I shall underline, a little clumsily, a number of axiomatic trivialities or a number of presuppositions. I have every reason to suppose that, with regard to each of these it would be easy to reach an initial consensus between us, even if I still intend to undermine the conditions of this consensus at a later stage. In order to invoke this consensus I refer, perhaps imprudently, to our commonality as subjects sharing, for the most part, in the same culture, and subscribing, within a given context, to the same system of conventions. Which?

This is the first belief that has an axiomatic appearance: we acknowledge that the text we have just read has its own identity, a singularity and a unity. We judge them, in advance, to be untouchable, even though, at the end of the day, the conditions of this self-identity, this singularity and this unity, remain enigmatic. There is a beginning and an end to this narrative whose borders or limits seem to us to be guaranteed by a certain number of established *criteria*, that is to say established by positive laws and conventions. We hold that this text is unique and identical with itself, we presuppose that it exists in its original version and that, in its birthplace, it is of a piece with the German language. According to the most widespread belief in these regions, that version we call original constitutes the ultimate point of reference with regard to what might be

---

34. [Franz Kafka, "Before the Law," trans. Willa and Edwin Muir, in *The Complete Short Stories of Franz Kafka,* ed. N. N. Glatzer (London: Vintage, 2005), 3–4.—Trans.]

called the juridical personality of the text, its identity, its unicity, its rights, etc. Today, all of that is guaranteed by a cluster of laws that have their own history, even if the discourse that justifies them generally claims that they are rooted in natural laws.

The second element on which there is axiomatic consensus, which is essentially inseparable from the first: this text has an author. The existence of its signatory is not fictitious, unlike the characters in the narrative. And once more it is the law that requires and guarantees the difference between the *presumed* reality of the author, bearing the name Franz Kafka, registered by the registry office under the authority of the state, and on the other hand the fiction of the characters within the narrative. This difference implies a system of laws and conventions without which the consensus to which I am now referring, in a context that (up to a certain point) we share, would have no chance of becoming visible, whether or not it is founded. Now this system of laws: we can know at least its apparent history, the juridical events that have marked its evolution in the form of positive law. This history of conventions is very recent, and anything guaranteed by it remains essentially subject to change, as fragile as an ingenious trick. As you know, we have been bequeathed some works whose unity, identity, and completeness remain problematic because nothing allows us to decide with certainty if the incompleteness of the corpus is an accident or a trick, a deliberately calculated sham on the part of one or more authors, whether contemporary or not. There are and there have been works in which the author or a multiplicity of authors are presented as characters, though we are not given rigorous signs or criteria to distinguish between the two functions or the two values. The *Tale of the Grail,* for example, still poses such problems today (completeness or incompleteness, real or feigned incompleteness, authors inscribed within the narrative, pseudonymity and literary ownership, etc.).[35] But, without wishing to eradicate the differences and the historical mutations on this matter, we can be sure that, in line with the modalities that are original on each occasion, these problems have always been posed and for every work.

Third axiom or presupposition: there is narrative [*il y a du récit*] in this text entitled "Before the Law" and the narrative belongs to what we call literature. There is a narrative or a narrative form in this text; the narration draws everything in its train, it determines every atom of the text even if everything in it does not immediately seem to belong to the species of narration. Leaving aside the question of whether this narrativity is the genre, the mode, or the type of the text,[36] I will note modestly and in an entirely preliminary way that this narrativity, in this specific case, belongs, in my view, to literature; in support of that I invoke once more the same preexisting consensus that we share. Without saying anything more about the contextual presuppositions of our consensus, I note that, in my view, we seem to be dealing with a literary narrative (the word "narrative" [*récit*] also poses translation difficulties that I am leaving to one side).[37] Is that too obvious or trivial to be worthy of mention? I do not think so. Certain narratives do not belong to literature, for example historical chronicles or those things that are related to us in our everyday

---

35. On all these questions (real or feigned incompleteness, plurality of authors' "literary ownership [which] it seems did not pose, or almost did not pose a problem in the Middle Ages" (at 52), I refer you to the most recent and the richest work, Roger Dragonetti, *La vie de la lettre au Moyen Age (Le conte du Graal)* (Paris: Le Seuil, 1980).

36. Cf. Gérard Genette, "Genres, 'types,' modes," *Poétique* 32 (1977): 389–421, reproduced with some modifications in Gérard Genette, *Introduction à l'architexte* (Paris: Seuil, 1979) [see Gérard Genette, *The Architect: An Introduction,* trans. Jane E. Lewin (Berkeley: University of California Press, 1992).—Trans.].

37. [See note 25 above on *récit*.—Trans.]

lives: so, for example, I can tell you that I appeared before the law after being photographed at the wheel of my car, at night, driving in my neighborhood in excess of the speed limit, or that I was going to appear before the law, in Prague, and be accused of drug trafficking. So it is not because it is a narrative that we understand "Before the Law" to be a literary phenomenon. If we judge that the text is "literary," this is also not because the narrative is fictional, allegorical, mythical, symbolical, parabolical, etc. There are fictions, allegories, myths, symbols, or parables that have nothing about them that is properly literary. So what is it that determines the fact that "Before the Law" belongs to what we think we understand by the term "literature"? And who makes that determination? Who judges? In order to sharpen up to these two questions (what? and who?), I wish to make it clear that I am not giving preference to either of them and that they are understood in relation to literature rather than to belles-lettres, poetry, or the art of discourse in general, even though all these distinctions remain highly problematic.

The double question would therefore be the following: "Who decides, who judges, and according to which criteria whether this narrative [récit] belongs to literature?"

In order not to take liberties with the time available, which I must bear in mind, I will say immediately and quite plainly that I am giving, and that I have, no answer to such a question. Jean-François Lyotard would say, I am "without a criterion." You will perhaps think that I wish to lead you to a purely aporetic conclusion or, in any event, to a problematic exaggeration: in that case one might say that the question is badly framed, that it is not possible to argue in terms of belonging to a field or a class where literature is concerned, that literature has no essence, no domain that is properly literary and rigorously identifiable as such, and, finally, since the term "literature" will forever remain improper, having no concept, no guaranteed reference, no

28

criteria, that "literature" would have something to do with the drama surrounding the name, the law of the name, and the name of the law. You would certainly not be wrong. But the generality of these laws and these problematic conclusions interests me less than the singularity of a trial that, in the course of a unique drama, forces them to appear before an irreplaceable corpus, before this very text, before "Before the Law." There is a singularity about the relationship to the law, a law of singularity that is obliged to establish a relationship without ever being able to do so as regards the general or universal essence of the law. Now you will have noticed already that this specific text, this singular text names or relates in its own way that conflict without encounter between law and singularity, that *paradox* or that *enigma* of the being-before-the-law; and often, in Greek, *ainigma* is a relation, a narrative, the obscure word of an apologue:"These are difficulties the man from the country has not expected. The law, he thinks, should surely be accessible at all times and to everyone . . . ." And the reply, if we may speak it yet, comes at the end of the narrative, which also marks the end of the man:"The doorkeeper recognizes that the man has reached his end, and, to let his failing senses catch the words, roars in his ear:'No one else could ever be admitted here, since this gate was made only for you. I am now going to shut it.'"[38]

My ambition would therefore be simply to sharpen, at the risk of deforming, the double question (who decides, who judges, and on what grounds whether this narrative belongs to literature?) and above all to bring the enunciation of this double question before the law, or even (as is readily said in French these days), the subject of its

---

38. [The German reads:"Ich gehe jetzt und schließe ihn (I am leaving now, and closing it)."The French translation that Derrida relies on is here closer to the German than the English translation reproduced above.—Trans.]

enunciation. Such a subject would lay claim to reading and understanding the text entitled "Before the Law," and the subject would read it as a narrative and would classify it conventionally in the field of literature. He would think that he knew what literature is and, thus armed, would ask himself only: What is it that allows me to determine that this narrative is a literary phenomenon? Or to judge it in the category "literature"?

The task is therefore to summon this question, the subject of the question and its system of axioms or conventions, to appear "before the law," before "Before the Law." What does that mean?

We cannot here alter the specificity [*singularité*] of the language. To appear before the law, in the French, German, or English languages means to come or to be brought before the judges, the representatives or the guardians of the law, in a trial, and there to act as a witness or to be judged. The trial, the judgment (*Urteil*), that is, the place, the site, the situation, that is what is necessary in order for such an event to take place, "to appear before the law."

Here the expression "Before the Law," which I put in inverted commas, is the title of a narrative. This is the fourth of our axiomatic presuppositions. I must add it to our list. We believe we know what a title is, particularly the title of a work. It is placed in a certain place that is precisely determined and prescribed by the laws of convention: before and above, at a prescribed distance from the body of the text, and certainly *before* it. The title is generally chosen by the author or his editorial representatives who have ownership of it. The title names and guarantees the identity, the unity, and the limits of the original work that bears its title. It goes without saying that the powers and the value of a title have an essential relationship to something such as the law, whether it is a title in general that is in question, or the title of a work, whether this is literary or not. There is already a sort of intrigue perceptible in a title that names the law ("Before the Law"), as though the law were giving a title to itself or as though the word "title" were introducing itself insidiously into the title. In saying this I am perhaps locating myself in the margin of what is written in *Duchamp's TRANS/formers*:"Decisions residing in the title," the title itself, says Lyotard, is "converted into two subtitles: 'Given the illuminating [lamplight] gas' and 'Given the Waterfall'" (174 and 175). Let us simply wait for this intrigue.

Let me emphasize topology. Another intriguing aspect: the sense of the title represents a topological indication, *before the law*. And the same utterance, the same name (because the title is a name), at any event the same group of words, would not function as a title if they appeared elsewhere, in places that are not prescribed by convention. They would not function as a title if they appeared in another context or in another place within the same context. For example, right here the expression *Vor dem Gesetz* is presented the first time (or, if you prefer, the second time) as the incipit of the narrative. It is the opening sentence:"Vor dem Gesetz steht ein Türhüter," "Before the law there is (or there stands) a guardian of the gate," a gatekeeper. Although we might suppose they have the same sense, they are homonyms rather than synonyms, because the two occurrences of the same expression do not name the same thing; they do not refer to the same thing and do not have the same value. On opposite sides of the invisible line that separates the title from the text, the one names the entirety of the text of which it is the overall name and title, the other designates a situation, the location of the character situated within the interior geography of the narrative. One, the title, is located *before* the text and remains external, if not to the fiction, at least to the content of the fictional narration. The other is also located at the head of the text, before it but already within it; it is an initial interior element of the fictional content

31

of the narration. And yet, although it is external to the fictional narration, to the story told by the narrative, the title ("Before the Law") remains a fiction that is also signed by the author or by his representative. The title belongs to literature, we would say, even if its belonging has neither the structure nor the status of that to which it gives a title and in relation to which it remains essentially heterogeneous. The fact that the title belongs to literature does not prevent it from having legal authority. For example, the title of a book makes possible its classification in a library, the attribution of copyright and rights of ownership, the legal proceedings and the judgments that can flow from that, etc. Nevertheless, this function does not operate in the same way as the title of a nonliterary work, such as a treatise on physics or law.

The reading of "Before the Law" that I am now going to attempt will be shaped by two programs, if one might put it thus, and therefore (pragmatically) by two destinations. The first destination exactly [*au juste*] makes us address each other, or in the name of Jean-François Lyotard, whom we are not sure that we really [*au juste*] know, or that we know what he wants, or how to judge him, even though he seems, for example (I say for example in order not to delay you for hours with quotations), to have signed this passage that deals with the "pragmatics of Judaism" in *Au Juste*,[39] as I am also going to do, though more indirectly and more hypothetically:

> God commands. One does not know very well what he commands. He commands obedience, that is, that one place oneself in the position of the pragmatic genre of obligation . . . . We call that [*ça*] God, but ultimately we do not know what we are saying when we say God. We know nothing about it [*ça*]. We merely

---

39. [Lyotard and Thébaud, *Just Gaming*, 52. —Trans.]

say: There is a law. And when we say "law," it does not mean that the law is defined and that it suffices to abide by it. There is a law, but we do not know what this law says. There is a kind of law of laws, there is a metalaw that says "be just." That is all that matters in Judaism: "Be just." But we do not know what it is to be just. That is, we have to be "just." It is not "Abide by this"; it is not "love one another," etc. All of that is child's play. "Be just"; case by case, every time it will be necessary to decide, to commit oneself, to judge, and then to meditate if that was just.

There it is: that is what I am going to speak about in this reading of Kafka. I do not know if all the Jews—and even the experts in Judaism, even Levinas, whom he invokes a few lines further on—would recognize themselves in this analysis of the paradoxical Jewish pragmatics, but that is not a criterion. If I, for my part, recognized myself in it, that would reassure neither the Jews nor the others, and in fact that does not matter. In any case I would be quite tempted to recognize Lyotard in it, or "my" Lyotard, and that includes whatever he might have said that was to be said about the law and about the being-before the law.

The other destination of this reading will have been marked by a seminar during which, last year, I believe I harassed [*harceler*] this narrative by Kafka. In truth it is he who laid siege to the ideas that I was working out on the moral law and respect for the law in the Kantian doctrine of practical reason, on the thinking of Heidegger and Freud in their relation to the moral law and respect (in the Kantian sense). I cannot here reconstitute the modes and the trajectories of that harassment. To indicate the principal headings and *topoi*, let us say that it was concerned in the first place with the strange status of the example, the symbol, and the type in Kantian doctrine. As you know, Kant speaks of a *typic* [*typique*] and not of a schema of practical reason;[40] of a *symbolic* presentation of moral goodness (the beautiful as a symbol of morality in paragraph 59 of the *Critique of Judgment*); and also of a respect that, if it is never directed at things, is nevertheless directed at people only in so far as they provide an *example* of the moral law: respect is due only to the moral law, which is the only cause of it even though that moral law never presents itself. I was also dealing with the "as if" (*als ob*) in the second formulation of the categorical imperative: "Act as though the maxim of your action were to become by your will a universal law of nature."[41] This "as if" makes it possible to align practical reason with a historical teleology and with the possibility of infinite progress. I was trying to show how he introduced narrativity and fiction virtually into the very heart of his thought on law, at the very moment when law begins to speak and to question the moral subject. Precisely when the authority of the law seems to exclude any historicity and any empirical narrativity, at the moment when its rationality seems alien to fiction and imagination of any kind (even the transcendental imagination),[42] it seems a priori to still offer its hospitality to these parasites. Two other motifs had also caught my attention, among those that have some bearing on Kafka's narrative: the motif of the lofty and the sublime that plays an essential role in it, and then the motif of the

---

40. [See Immanuel Kant, *Critique of Practical Reason,* trans. and ed. Mary Gregor (Cambridge: Cambridge University Press, 2006), 58–62.—Trans.]

41. [See Immanuel Kant, *Groundwork for the Metaphysics of Morals,* trans. Arnulf Zweig (Oxford: Oxford University Press, 2002), 222 (par 4: 421).—Trans.]

42. It is here that the seminar had interrogated the Heideggerian interpretation of "respect" in its relation to the transcendental imagination. Cf. Martin Heidegger, *Kant and the Problem of Metaphysics,* 5th ed., trans. Richard Taft (Bloomington: Indiana University Press, 1997), especially around §30.

guard and the guardian.[43] I cannot deal with this at length; I am giving only a broad outline of the context in which I read "Before the Law." It is a space in which it is difficult to say whether Kafka's narrative offers a powerful philosophical ellipsis, or if pure practical reason guards within itself an element of the fantastical or of narrative fiction. One of those questions might be: What if law, even if it is not through and through literature, shared its conditions of possibility with the literary thing [*la chose littéraire*]?[44]

In order to give it, here, today, its most economical formulation I will speak of the *appearance* of the narrative and of law, that appear, appear together and see themselves summoned the one before the other: the narrative, that is to say a certain type of *relation,* refers to the law that it relates, and in so doing it appears before the law, which appears before it. And yet, as we shall see when we read, nothing is really presented in this appearance; and the fact that we are given it to read does not signify that we will have the proof or the experience of it.

The law as such, apparently, should never give rise to any narrative. In order to be invested with its categorical authority, the law should have no history, no genesis, no derivation whatever. That would be the law of law. Pure morality has no history, and that is what Kant initially seems to remind us of, no intrinsic history (or then, as Lyotard says, history can be only the "to do" [*"à-faire"*] of the future, and that is perhaps as close to Heidegger as it is to Levinas, at least in this form). And when stories are told about it, they

---

43. Among other examples: at the end of *The Critique of Practical Reason,* philosophy is presented as the guardian *(Aufbewahrerin)* of the pure science of morals; it is also the "narrow gate" *(enge Pforte)* leading to the doctrine of wisdom.

44. [For an analysis of "the thing," see Derrida, *Signéponge/Signsponge*; and *The Truth in Painting,* trans. Geoff Bennington and Ian McLeod (Chicago: The University of Chicago Press, 1987). —Trans.]

can be only about circumstances, events that are external to the law, at the very most modes by which it is revealed. As the man from the country in Kafka's narrative, narrative relations would try to get close to the law, to make it present, to enter into a relationship with it, even to enter into it, to become *intrinsic* to it, but that is not possible. The narrative of these maneuvers would be only the narrative of what escapes the narrative and which, finally, remains inaccessible to it. But the inaccessible provokes, even in its hiding place. One cannot have anything to do with law, with the law of laws, either from up close or from afar, without asking (oneself) where is its proper place and where does it come from. I say again "the law of laws" because, in Kafka's narrative, we do not know what sort of law we are dealing with, the law of morality, of law or of politics, even of nature, and so forth. This is what remains invisible and hidden in each law, so one might suppose that it is the law itself, the law that causes these laws to be laws, the being-law of these laws. The question and the quest are unavoidable, or in other terms, the itinerary toward the place and the origin of law. The latter reveals itself whilst withholding itself [*se donne en se refusant*], acknowledging neither its origin nor its location. This silence and this discontinuity constitute the phenomenon of law. Entering into a relationship with law, with the law that says "You must" and "You must not," is also to behave as if law had no history or at least did not depend on its historical presentation; and it is at the same time to be fascinated, provoked, addressed by the history of this nonhistory. It is to be tempted by the impossible: a theory of the origin of law, and therefore of its nonorigin, for example, of the moral law. Freud (Kafka read him as you know, but this Austro-Hungarian law dating from the beginning of the century is of little importance), invented the concept, if not the word, "repression" as a reply to the question of the origin of the moral law. That was before Kafka wrote "Vor dem Gesetz"

(1919), but that relationship is of no interest to us, and dates from more than twenty-five years before the Second Topography and the theory of the Superego. As early as his letters to Fliess he relates the narrative [*récit*] of presentiments and premonitions with a sort of anxious fervor, as though he were on the brink of a revelation: "Another presentiment tells me, *as though I already knew* [emphasis added, *J.D.*]—but I know nothing at all—that I shall very soon uncover the source of morality."[45] There then follow a few narratives [*récits*] of dreams and, four months later, another letter declares "the certain insight that there are no indications of reality in the unconscious, so that one cannot distinguish between truth and fiction that has been cathected with affect."[46] A few weeks later there is another letter, from which I extract the following lines: "after the frightful labor pains of the last few weeks, I gave birth to a new piece of knowledge. Not entirely new, to tell the truth; it had repeatedly shown itself and withdrawn again; but this time it stayed and looked upon the light of day. Strangely enough, I have a presentiment of such events a good while beforehand. For instance, I wrote to you once in the summer that I was going to find the source of normal sexual repression (morality, shame, and so forth) and then for a long time failed to find it. Before the vacation trip I told you that the most important patient for me was myself; and then, after I came back from vacation, my self-analysis, of which there was at the time no sign, suddenly started. A few weeks ago came my wish that repression might be replaced by my knowledge of the essential thing *lying behind it* [emphasis added, *J.D.*]; and that is what I

---

45. Letter of May 31, 1897. [Sigmund Freud, *The Complete Letters of Sigmund Freud to Wilhelm Fliess, 1887–1904,* trans. Jeffrey M. Masson (Cambridge, Mass.: The Belknap Press of Harvard University Press, 1985), 249.—Trans.]

46. Letter of September 21, 1897. [Freud, 264.—Trans.]

am concerned with now."[47] Freud then moves on to consider the concept of repression, the hypothesis that it is organically linked to standing upright or, to put it another way, to a certain *elevation*.[48] The move to standing upright lifts or raises man and distances his nose from the anal and genital sexual zones. This distancing ennobles height and leaves traces by virtue of the fact that it defers action [*différant l'action*]. Postponement, *différance,* ennobling elevation, the sense of smell turned away from the stench of sexuality, repression: that is the origin of morality. "To put it crudely, the memory actually stinks just as in the present the object stinks; and in the same manner as we turn away our sense organ (the head and nose) in disgust, the preconscious and the sense of consciousness turn away from the memory. This is *repression.* What now, does normal repression furnish us with? Something which, free, can lead to anxiety; if physically bound, to rejection—that is to say, the affective basis for a multitude of intellectual processes of development, such as morality, shame, and the like. Thus the whole of this arises at the expense of (extinct) sexuality."[49]

However poor this initial understanding of repression might be, the only example of "intellectual processes" that Freud gives is the moral law or modesty. The schema of elevation, of upward movement, everything that is indicated by the preposition *sur (über)*[50] is in this case just as determinant as the schema of purification, of the turning away

47. Letter of November 14, 1897. [Freud, 278-79.—Trans.]

48. This argument should be linked to what he says later about Kant, concerning the categorical imperative, the moral law in our hearts and the starry heavens above our heads.

49. Letter of November 14, 1897. [Freud, *Letters to Fliess,* 280.—Trans.]

50. [Derrida appears to allude here to the above-mentioned superego (the *Über-Ich,* the *Surmoi).*—Trans.]

from all that is impure, from those zones of the body that smell unpleasant and must not be touched. This turning away is upward. The high (and therefore great) and the pure, that is what would be produced by repression when seen as the origin of morality, that is what is absolutely *better*, the origin of value and of our judgment about value. This becomes explicit in the *Project for a Scientific Psychology*, and then in other references to the Categorical Imperative, to the starry heavens above our heads, etc.

So, like many others, Freud wanted, from the outset, to write a history of law. He was on the track of law, and he recounts to Fliess his own history (which he calls his auto-analysis), the history of the route that he is following on the track of law. He was intuiting [*flairait*] the origin of law, and to do that he had to intuit intuition [*flairer le flair*].[51] The sum total is that he was beginning a grand narrative, and also an interminable auto-analysis, to relate, to give an account of the origin of law or, put another way, of the origin of that which, cut off from its origin, interrupts the genealogical narrative. Law is intolerant with regard to its own history, it intervenes like an order that presents itself as an absolute, absolute and detached from any origin. It appears as that which does not appear as itself in the course of a history. At all events, it does not permit itself to be constituted by a history that would give rise to a narrative. If there were a history, it would be neither presentable nor narratable, the history of what has not taken place.

Freud had sensed [*l'avait senti*] this, he had the nose for it, and had even (as he put it) experienced a presentiment about it. And he said it to Fliess, with whom an unnarratable history of the nose played out until the end of

---

51. [The French *flairer* also means to sniff, smell, scent, or sense.— Trans.]

their friendship, marked by the sending of a final post card of just two lines.[52] If we had continued in that direction it would also have been necessary to speak about the shape of the nose, whether it protruded or was pointed. There has been much talk of this theory among psychoanalysts, but perhaps insufficient attention has been paid to the presence of hairs in the nostrils, which do not hide themselves with sufficient modesty and which sometimes have to be cut.

If now, ignoring completely any relationship between Freud and Kafka, you place yourself before "Before the Law," and before the guardian of the gate, the *Türhüter*, and if, camped before him, like the man from the country, you look around, what do you see? By what detail, if one might put it this way, are you so fascinated that you isolate and select that particular feature? Well, by the abundance of the hairy decoration, whether natural or artificial, around pointed shapes, and particularly around the nasal protuberance. All of that is very dark, and the nose comes to symbolize along with the genital area, which we always associate with murky colors even if it is not always dark. Because of his situation, the man from the country does not know the law that is always the law of the city, the law of towns and buildings, of protected constructions, of gates and fences, of areas shut off by gates. So he is surprised by the guardian of the law, a man from the city, and he stares at him: "These are difficulties the man from the country has not expected. The law, he thinks, should surely

---

52. Fliess published in 1897 a work on the relations between the nose and the female sexual organs [Wilhelm Fliess, *Die Beziehungen zwischen Nase und weiblichen Geschlechtsorganen* (Leipzig: Deuticke).—Trans.]. An otolaryngologist, he greatly valued, as we know, his speculations on the nose and bisexuality, on the analogy between the nasal mucosa and the genital mucosa, in both men and women, on the swelling of the nasal mucosa and the rhythm of menstruation.

be accessible at all times and to everyone, but as he now takes a closer look (*genauer*) at the doorkeeper in his fur coat [*in seinem Pelzmantel*: the artificial ornamental hair, that of the city and the law, which will add to the natural hair], with his big sharp nose [*seine grosse Spitznase*, the "size" is omitted from the French translation] and long, thin, black Tartar beard [*den langen, dünnen, schwarzen tatarischen Bart*], he decides that it is better to wait [literally: he decides to prefer to wait, *entschliesst er sich, doch lieber zu warten, bis er die Erlaubnis zum Eintritt bekommt*] until he gets permission to enter."[53]

The scansion of this sequence is very clear. Even if it appears to be simply a narrative and chronological juxtaposition, the very relationship between these elements and the selection of the notations leads to a logical inference. The grammatical structure of the sentence gives rise to a thought: but (from the moment) when [*als*, as, at the moment when] the man from the country sees the guardian with his long pointed nose and the abundance of black hair, he makes up his mind to wait, he judges that it is better to wait. It is in fact at the sight of this hairy promontory, faced with a thick black forest surrounding an outcrop, a summit, or a nasal protuberance that, as a consequence that is both strange and entirely simple, entirely natural (one might even say *uncanny*,* *unheimlich*), the man makes up his mind, he decides. Because he is also a

---

53. [In Kafka's notebooks an inscription appears that suggests he also considered other possibilities in this respect: "I ran past the first watchman. Then I was horrified, ran back again and said to the watchman: 'I ran through here while you were looking the other way.' The watchman gazed ahead of him and said nothing. 'I suppose I really oughtn't to have done it,' I said. The watchman still said nothing. 'Does your silence indicate permission to pass?'"; see Franz Kafka, *Wedding Preparations in the Country and Other Posthumous Prose Writings,* trans. Ernst Kaiser and Eithne Wilkins (London: Secker & Warburg, 1954) 354-55.—Trans.]

determined man. Does he decide not to enter after having apparently decided to enter? Not at all. He decides not to decide yet, he decides to not make up his mind, he makes up his mind not to decide, he postpones, he delays, while he waits. But while he is waiting for what? "Permission to enter," as it says? But you have noticed, this permission was refused only in the form of a postponement: "It is possible, but not now."

We should be patient, too. Do not think that I am insisting on this narrative in order to lead you astray or to make you wait, in the antechamber of literature or fiction, for a properly philosophical treatment of the question of law, of respect before the law or of the categorical imperative. That which brings us, like the man from the country, to a standstill before the law is it not the same as that which paralyses us and holds us in suspense before a narrative, its possibility and its impossibility, its readability and its non-readability, its necessity and its prohibition, and all of that also in relation to its telling, its repetition, and its history?

When first encountered that seems to be a consequence of the essentially inaccessible nature of law, of the fact that when "first encountered" it is always refused, as the doubling of the title and the incipit already suggest. In a certain way, "Vor dem Gesetz" is the narrative of this inaccessibility, of this inaccessibility to the narrative, the history [*l'histoire*] of this impossible history, the map of this forbidden journey: no itinerary, no method, no pathway by which to reach the law, to reach what would happen there, to reach the *topos* of its event. Such inaccessibility astonishes the man from the country at the moment when he looks, at the instant when he observes the guardian who is himself the observer, the overseer, the sentinel, the very incarnation of vigilance, one could even say of conscience [*la conscience*]. The question put by the man from the country is simply about the pathway that gives access: is not law defined precisely by its accessibility? Is it not, *must* it not

42

be accessible "at all times and to everyone"? At this point the problem of exemplarity could be developed, particularly the Kantian concept of "respect": respect is nothing but the *effect* of the law, Kant emphasizes, it is due only to the law, and in the law [*en droit*] it appears only *before the law*; it is addressed to people only in so far as they provide an example of the fact that a law can be respected. It is thus never possible to have access *directly* either to people or to the law, one is never *immediately* before either of these entities—and the detour can be infinite. The very universality of law overflows all finitude and is therefore the cause of this risk.

But let us leave aside what would distract us from our narrative.

The man from the country thinks that the law should be accessible at all times and to everyone. It should be universal. Correspondingly, we say in French "*nul n'est censé ignorer la loi,*"[54] in this case, of positive law. No one is supposed to be ignorant of it, provided they are not illiterate, that they are able to read the text of the law or to delegate the reading and the capacity to a lawyer, to a man who represents the law. Unless being able to read were to make the law even more inaccessible. The reading of a text can in fact reveal that it is untouchable, truly intangible, *because it can be read,* and at the same time illegible in so far as the presence within it of a sense that is perceptible, graspable, remains as hidden as its origin. Illegibility is then no longer opposed to legibility. And perhaps man is a man from the country in so far as he is unable to read or, if he can read, he still has to deal with the illegibility within that which seems to allow itself to be read. He wishes to see or to touch the law, he wishes to approach it, to "enter" it because he is perhaps unaware that law is not a thing to

---

54. [Ignorance of the law is no excuse, or literally: no one is considered (to be) ignorant of the law.—Trans.]

be seen or touched but to be deciphered. This is perhaps the first sign of its inaccessibility or of the delay that it imposes on the man from the country. The gate is not closed, it is "open," "as always" (the text says), but the law remains inaccessible and, if that prohibits or bars the gateway to its genealogical history, by the same token it also keeps in suspense both the desire for an origin and the genealogical impulsion; which lose their impetus when faced with the procreation of the law, just as they do with parental procreation. Historical research leads the *relation* toward the impossible exhibiting of a site or an event, of a taking-place where law emerges as prohibition.

The law as prohibition—I abandon the expression, and leave it in suspension while I make a detour.

When Freud goes beyond his initial outline of the origin of morality, when he names the categorical imperative in the Kantian sense, he does so within an outline that appears to be historical. A narrative refers back to the singular historicity of an event, specifically to the murder of the primitive father. The conclusion of *Totem and Taboo* (1912)[55] states this clearly: "The earliest moral precepts and restrictions in primitive society have been explained by us as reactions to a deed which gave those who performed it the concept of 'crime.' They felt remorse for this deed [but how and why if this took place *before* morality, *before* the law? *J.D.*], and decided that it should never be repeated and that its performance should bring no advantage. This creative sense of guilt still persists among us. We find it operating in an asocial manner in neurotics, and producing new moral precepts and persistent restrictions, as an atonement for crimes that have been committed and as a precaution against the committing of new ones" (159). Speaking next about the totemic meal and

---

55. [See Freud, *The Standard Edition*, 13:1–161. Further page citations appear in the text.—Trans.]

about "mankind's earliest festival" (142) commemorating the murder of the father and the origin of morality, Freud insists on the ambivalence of the sons with regard to the father; in what I can reasonably call a movement of repentance, he adds a note of his own. It is very significant for me. It explains the overflowing of tenderness as a consequence of the increase in horror conferred on the crime by the fact of its complete pointlessness. "Not one of the sons had in fact been able to put his original wish—of taking the father's place—into effect" (143 n. 1). The murder fails because the dead father wields even greater power. Is the best way to kill him, not to keep him alive (finite)? And is the best way to keep him alive, not to murder him? Now failure, Freud specifies, promotes moral action. Morality is therefore born from a pointless crime that, at bottom, kills no one, that occurs too soon or too late, that puts an end to no power, and that, in truth, inaugurates nothing since it would have been necessary for repentance, and therefore morality, to have been *already* possible before the crime. Freud seems to hold to the reality of an event, but this event is a sort of nonevent, an event about nothing, a quasi-event that at the same time elicits and annuls the narrative relationship. The efficacy of the "deed" or the "misdeed" requires that, in some way, it should be interlaced with fiction. Everything happens as if.... For all that, the guilt is no less effective and painful: "The dead father became stronger than the living one had been—for events took the course we so often see them follow in human affairs to this day" (143). Given that the father is more powerful when dead than he had been during his life, given that he lives even more effectively as a result of his death and that, quite logically, he will have been dead while he was alive, more dead while living than *post mortem,* the murder of the father is not an event in the ordinary sense of the word. No more is the origin of the moral law. No one will have encountered it in its proper place, no one will have faced it in its taking-place. Event without event, pure event where nothing happens, eventiality [*événementialité*] of an event,[56] which requires and annuls the narrative in its fiction. Nothing new happens and yet this nothing new inaugurated the law, the two fundamental prohibitions of totemism, murder and incest. This event, which is both pure and a pure assumption, nevertheless marks an invisible rupture in history. It resembles a fiction, a myth or a fable; its narrative is structured in such a way that all the questions asked about Freud's intention are both inevitable and yet entirely without pertinence ("Did he really believe it or not?" "Did he maintain that we are dealing with a historical and real murder?" etc.). The structure of this event is such that we have neither to believe it nor not to believe it. Just like the question of belief, the question of the reality of its historical referent is, if not wiped out, at least irremediably fissured. Both calling forth and refusing the narrative, this quasi-event is marked by fictitious narrativity (fiction *of* a narration as much as fiction as narration: fictitious narration as simulacrum of narration and not simply as the narration of an imaginary story [*histoire*]). This is the origin of literature as well as the origin of law, like the dead father, a story that is told, a rumor doing the rounds, without an author or an end, but an inevitable and unforgettable narrative [*récit*]. Whether this is fantastical or not, whether it is a product of the imagination or not, even of the transcendental imagination, whether it speaks or says nothing about the origin of the fantasy, that takes nothing away from the imperious necessity of being spoken, takes nothing away from its law. This law is even more frightening, fantastical, *unheimlich, uncanny,** than if it emanated from pure reason, unless pure reason were in fact in league with an unconscious fantastic [*fantastique inconsciente*].

---

56. [In translations of Derrida's texts, *événementialité* is translated either as "eventness" or as "eventuality".—Trans.]

As early as 1897, and I am quoting again, Freud spoke of his "certain insight that there are no indications of reality in the unconscious, so that one cannot distinguish between truth and fiction that has been cathected with affect."[57]

If the law is fantastical, if its original location and its taking-place partake of the fabulous, it is understandable that "*das Gesetz*" should remain essentially inaccessible even when it, the law, presents itself or promises itself. From being a quest to reach it, to stand before it, respectfully face to face, to be introduced to it and into it, the narrative becomes the impossible narrative of the impossible. The narrative of prohibition is a prohibited narrative.

Did the man from the country want to enter into the law or only into the place where law shields itself? This is not clear; the alternative is perhaps spurious [*fausse*] since the law is itself a sort of place, a *topos* and a taking-place. In any case the man from the country (who is also a man who *pre-dates the law* [*d'avant la loi*], just as nature predates the city) does not want to remain before the law, in the position of the guardian. The latter also stands *before the law.* It could mean that he respects it: to stand before the law, to appear before it, is to submit oneself to it, to respect it, all the more so because respect keeps at a distance, upholds an opposing position [*maintient en face*] and forbids contact or penetration. But it can also mean that, standing before the law, the guardian causes it to be respected. Tasked with keeping a lookout, he therefore mounts guard *before it* by turning his back to it, without facing it, without being "*in front*" *of it,** the sentinel who keeps a lookout over the entrances to the building and imposes respect on the visitors who *present* themselves before the castle. The inscription "before the law" is therefore divided one more time. It was somehow already double by virtue of its textual

57. Letter of September 21, 1897. [Freud, *Letters to Fliess,* 264.— Trans.]

location, both title and *incipit*. It also splits in two again in respect of what it says and describes: a division of the territory and absolute opposition in the scene, with regard to the law. The two characters in the narrative, the guardian and the man from the country, are certainly before the law but, as they face each other to speak to each other, their position "before the law" is an opposition. One of the two, the guardian, turns his back on the law before which he nevertheless stands ("Vor dem Gesetz steht ein Türhüter"). The man from the country, on the other hand, also stands before the law, but in an opposite position, since it might be supposed that, being ready to enter, he faces it. The two protagonists are both positioned before the law, but they are opposed to each other on either side of a line of inversion signified in the text precisely by the separation of the title from the body of the narrative. A double inscription of "Vor dem Gesetz" around an invisible line, which divides, separates, and of itself makes a single expression divisible. The line subdivides the very nature of the expression [*Elle en dédouble le trait*].

This becomes possible only with the emergence of the entitling authority [*l'instance intitulante*] in its topical and juridical function. That is why I have taken an interest in the narrative bearing this title rather than a passage from *The Trial*, which tells more or less the same story but which, obviously, has no title. In German as in French, "before the law" is commonly understood in the sense of a subject who presents himself, respectfully and submissively, before the representatives or the guardians of the law. He presents himself before the representatives: the law in person, if one can put it this way, is never present, even though "before the law" seems to signify "in the presence of the law." The man therefore faces the law without ever being face to face with it. He can be *in front of it*,* he never confronts it. The first words of the incipit, latched onto a sentence, of which the title may be the

48

interrupted version ("Vor dem Gesetz," "Vor dem Gesetz steht ein Türhüter")[58]—begin to signify something quite different, and perhaps even the opposite of the title that nevertheless reproduces these first words, in the same way as certain poems are given a title that is the same as the beginning of the first line. The structure and the function of these two occurrences, of the two events of the same mark are, I repeat, certainly heterogeneous, but since these two different but identical events do not follow each other in a narrative sequence and are not logically consequential, it is impossible to say that the one *precedes* the other in any order whatever. They both come first in their order and neither of the two homonyms or, one might say, the two synonyms, quotes the other. The entitling event gives its law and its name to the text. Now this is an act of force. For example with respect to *The Trial,* from which he rips this narrative to make of it another institution. Without yet becoming involved in the narrative sequence, it opens a scene, makes way for a topographical system of law prescribing the two inverse and adverse positions, the antagonism of the two characters equally involved in it. The entitling sentence describes the one who turns his back on the law (to turn one's back is also to ignore, to refuse to acknowledge, even to transgress) not in order that the law might present itself or in order to be presented to it but on the contrary to forbid any presentation. And the one who faces sees no more than the one who turns his back. Neither of them is in the presence of the law. The only two characters in the narrative are blind and separated, separated from each other and separated from the law. Such is the modality of this rapport, of this relationship, of this narrative: blindness and separation, a sort of without-rapport. For, let us not forget, the guardian is also separated from the law by other guardians, "each," he says,

---

58. [There is no opening parenthesis in the French.—Trans.]

"more powerful than the last" ("einer mächtiger als der andere"): "I am powerful. And I am only the least of the doorkeepers [in the hierarchy, *der unterste*]. From hall to hall there is one doorkeeper after another, each more powerful than the last. The third doorkeeper is already so terrible that even I cannot bear to look at him" ("den Anblick . . . ertragen"). The last of the guardians is the first to see the man from the country. The first in the order of the narrative is the last in the order of the law and in the hierarchy of its representatives. And this first-last guardian never sees the law; he cannot even bear to look at the guardians who are *before* him (ahead of and above him). This is implicit in his title as guardian of the gate. And, for his part, clearly in sight, observed even by the man who, *on seeing him,* decides to decide nothing or judges that he does not need to make a decision [*qu'il n'a pas à arrêter son jugement*]. I say "the man" for the man from the country, as is the case sometimes in the narrative that, in this way, leaves the impression that the guardian, for his part, is perhaps not simply a man; and that this man is Man [*l'Homme*] as much as anyone else, the anonymous subject of the law. The man therefore makes up his mind that "it is better to wait" at the moment when his attention is drawn to the guardian's hairiness and to his pointed nose. His decision to make no decision brings about the narrative and causes it to continue. Permission, I pointed out, had apparently been refused, but in reality it had been delayed, postponed, put off. Everything is a question of time, the time of the narrative; but time itself appears only after this adjournment of presentation, after the law of the delay or the advance of the law, according to this anachrony in the relationship between them.

Law's prohibition at the present time is therefore not a prohibition, in the sense of an imperative constraint, it is a *différance.* Because, after having said "later," the guardian specifies, saying to him: "If you are so drawn to it, just try to go in despite my veto." Previously he had said to him "but not at the moment." But then he steps to one side and allows the man to stoop and peer through the gateway into the interior. It is stated that the gateway always remains open. It marks the boundary although it is itself not an obstacle or an enclosure [*clôture*]. It marks but has no consistency and is not opaque or uncrossable. It allows one to look into the interior ("in das Innere"), not at the law itself, of course, but the interior of spaces that are apparently empty and provisionally forbidden. The gateway is physically open, the guardian does not interpose himself by force. It is his words that are effective at this boundary, not to forbid directly, but to interrupt and delay entry or permission to enter. The man has the natural or physical freedom to enter into the interior, if not into the law. He must therefore, he must (it must be noted) forbid himself from entering. He must force himself, give himself the order, not to obey the law, but to not access [*ne pas accéder*] the law that, in effect, ensures that he is told or that he knows: Do not come to me, I order you not yet to come as far as me. It is there and in this that I am the law and that you will accede [*accéderas*] to my request. Without having access to me [*Sans accéder à moi*].

Because the law is interdiction. Noun and attribute. This would be the terrible *double-bind** of its very taking-place. It is interdiction: that does not signify that the law interdicts, but that it is itself interdicted, an interdicted space. The law interdicts and contradicts itself whilst placing the man in contradiction with himself:[59] we cannot reach it,

59. This contradiction is doubtless not the simple consequence of a law that, in itself, postulates and thereby produces transgression, the active or actual relationship with sin, with error. "Before the Law" perhaps invites us to read, somehow displaced to or trembling between the Old and the New Testaments, a text that is thus both archived and altered, I mean the Epistle to the Romans, chapter 7. It would be worth giving more time to the relationship between these

and in order to have some *rapport* with the law based on respect, *one must not, one must not* have any rapport with it, *the relationship must be interrupted.* We must *establish a relationship* only with its representatives, its examples, its guardians. And these are interrupters just as much as messengers. One must not know who the law is, what it is, where it is, where and how it is presented, where it comes from and from where it speaks. That is what *you must* do in response to the *you must* of the law. *Ci falt,* as they used to write in the Middle Ages at the end of a narrative.[60]

There you have the trial, the judgment, the process and *Urteil,* the originary division of law. The law is interdicted. But this contradictory auto-interdiction allows the man to act "freely" with self-determination, although this freedom cancels itself out as a self-imposed interdiction to enter into the law. Before the law, appearing before the law, the man is subject to the law. Of course. But *before* the law,

---

two texts. In it Paul reminds his brothers, "those who know the law," that "the law is binding on a person only during that person's lifetime." And Christ's death would be the death of the old law by which we "know" sin: having died with Christ, we are freed, absolved from that law, we are dead to that law, to the out-dated "letter" of that law in any case, and we serve it in a "new" spirit. And Paul adds that, when he was without the law, he lived; and when, with the law, the commandment came, he died [Romans 7: 1, 4, 9 (NRSV).—Trans.]

60. "*Ci falt*: this concluding utterance, by which a writer in the Middle Ages indicates the end of his work, before giving the title of it or his own name, does not appear, and for good reason, in *Le Conte du Graal,* an unfinished novel by Chrétien de Troyes. Derived from the Latin *fallere,* which gave 'faillir' ('to fall' and 'to deceive') and 'falloir' ('to lack'), the verb *falt* (or *faut*) acquired, in the Old French formula *ci falt,* the sense of 'here ends' without however losing the idea of 'lack' or 'failure.' Thus the work comes to a conclusion precisely where it is absent." Dragonetti, *Le conte du Graal,* 9. The thesis of this book, we might remind ourselves at this point, remains that "*Le Conte du Graal* was perfectly completed" (9).

because he cannot enter it, he is also *outside the law* [*hors la loi*]. He is neither under the law nor in the law. Subject of the law: outside the law. The man stooped down to see into the interior, which allows us to think that, in that moment, he is taller than the open door, and this question of height still awaits our consideration. After having observed the guardian more attentively, he makes up his mind to wait for permission, which is both given and postponed, but which the first guardian has caused him to believe will be indefinitely postponed. Behind the first guardian there are others, an unspecified number of others; perhaps there are more than can be counted, each more powerful than the last, and therefore increasingly able to interdict, strong in their ability to postpone. Their power is the *différance,* an unending *différance* since it lasts days, "years," and finally until the man's end. *Différance* until death, for death, without end because ended. As represented by the guardian, the words spoken by the law do not say "no" but "not yet," indefinitely. And from this stems the engagement in the narrative that is both perfectly ended and brutally interrupted, one might say primitively interrupted.

That which is deferred is not this or that experience, access to some pleasure [*une jouissance*], to something good, not even a supreme good, the possession or the penetration of something or of someone. That which is forever deferred, even until death, is entry into the law itself, which is nothing other than that which dictates the delay. By interfering and delaying [*en interférant et en différant*], the law interdicts the "doing" [*"férance"*], the rapport, the relationship, the reference [*référence*]. The origin of *différance,* that is what *one must not* and that cannot be approached, presented, represented, and above all, penetrated. That is the law of law, the trial of a law about which one can never say "there it is," here or there. It is neither natural nor institutional. One never arrives there and, ultimately within its original and its own taking-place, it never arrives. It is even more "sophisticated," if I can put it this way, than the convention governing the conventionalism that is conventionally attributed to the sophists. It is always cryptic, being both a secret that a caste—for example the nobility about which Kafka speaks in "The Problem of Our Laws"[61]—feigns to possess, and a delegation in favor of the secret. This secret is nothing—and this is the secret that must be well kept, it is not anything present or that can be presented, but this nothing must be carefully guarded, it must be guarded carefully. The nobility is delegated to this guard. The nobility is simply that and, as is suggested in "The Problem of Our Laws," the people would be taking a great risk if they deprived themselves of it. The people would understand nothing about the essence of the law. If the nobility is required, it is because this essence has no essence, because it can neither be nor be there. It is at one and the same time both obscene and unpresentable—and the nobles must be allowed to take responsibility for it. No one but a noble can do that. Except perhaps God.

Basically we have here a situation in which it is never a question of trial or judgment. Neither verdict[62] nor sentence, and that makes it all the more terrifying. What we have is the law, the law *that is not there but that there is* [*qui n'est pas là mais qu'il y a*]. As for judgment, it never arrives.[63] In this other sense, the man of nature is

---

61. [Kafka "The Problem of Our Laws," in *The Complete Short Stories,* 437-38.—Trans.]

62. [Kafka's "The Judgment" (*Das Urteil*) in *The Complete Short Stories,* 77, appears in French translation as "Le Verdict."—Trans.]

63. [The French *n'arrive pas* can also be translated as "it does not happen" or "it never happens." We opt here and elsewhere for "arrive" in view of the importance of the notion of "arrival" in Derrida's texts, or we provide the French in brackets; see e.g. Jacques Derrida, *The Post Card: From Socrates to Freud and Beyond,* trans. Alan Bass (Chicago: The University of Chicago Press, 1987); and *Aporias* (Stanford, Calif.: Stanford University Press, 1993), 33-35.—Trans.]

not merely the subject of the law outside the law, he is also, to infinity, but finitely, the prejudged [*le préjugé*]. Not in the sense of being judged in advance, but of being in advance of a judgment that is always in preparation and always delayed. Prejudged as though of necessity having to be judged [*devant être jugé*], preceding the law [*devaçant la loi*] that signifies, that (for him) signifies only "later."

And if that has to do with the essence of the law, it is because the law has no essence. It escapes from that essence of being that would consist in presence. Its "truth" is that nontruth, of which Heidegger says that it is the truth about truth.[64] As such, truth without truth, it *guards itself,* it guards itself without guarding itself, guarded by a guardian who guards nothing, since the gateway is open, and open on to nothing.[65] Like truth, the law might be simply the guard (*Wahrheit*), only the guard. And that special look [*regard singulier*] that passes between the guardian and the man.

But, beyond a look, beyond being (the law is nothing that might be present), the law calls in silence. Even before moral conscience as such, it requires a response, it is addressed to responsibility and to the guard. It sets in motion the guardian and the man, that singular couple, drawing them toward itself, and bringing them to a standstill before itself. It determines the being-toward-death before it. Another minute displacement and the guardian of the law (*Hüter*) would resemble the shepherd of being (*Hirt*).[66] I believe in the necessity of this "rapprochement," as it is called but, beneath the proximity, beneath the metonymy

---

64. [See e.g. Martin Heidegger, *Basic Writings,* ed. David Farrell Kell (New York: HarperSanFrancisco, 1993), 179–80 and 185–86, for the notion of truth as un-truth.—Trans.]

65. [Heidegger, 191–93, 196, 202, on the relation between truth and guarding/preserving.—Trans.]

66. [Heidegger, 234 and 245–46, on man as the shepherd of Being (*Hirt des Seins*).—Trans.]

perhaps (the law, another name for being; being, another name for the law; in both cases, the "transcendens" as Heidegger says of being),[67] the abyss of a difference still remains hidden and guarded.

The narrative (of what never happens) does not tell us what sort of law is thus manifested in its nonmanifestation: natural, moral, juridical, political? With regard to gender, it is grammatically neuter in German, *das Gesetz,* neither feminine nor masculine. In French the feminine brings about a semantic contagion that is not possible to forget, any more than it is possible to ignore language as a fundamental medium of law. In *The Madness of the Day,* by Maurice Blanchot,[68] it is possible to speak of an *appearance* of the law, in the form of a feminine "silhouette": neither a man nor a woman but a feminine silhouette that becomes a couple with the quasi-narrator of a forbidden or impossible narrative (that is the whole narrative of this nonnarrative). The "I" of the narrator frightens the law. It is the law that appears to take fright and that retreats. As for the narrator, in another analogy that is unrelated to "Before the Law," he tells how he was obliged to appear before representatives of the law (police officers, judges, or doctors), men who required a narrative of him. That narrative he could not give, but it turns out to be the very narrative that he proposes in order to relate the impossible.

Here, *das Gesetz,* we do not know *what* it is, we are unaware of *who* it is. And thus perhaps literature begins. A philosophical, scientific, or historical text, a text conveying knowledge or information, would not just give [*abandonnerait*] a name to nonknowledge, or at least would do

---

67. [Heidegger, *Being and Time,* 62.—Trans.]

68. [See Maurice Blanchot, *The Station Hill Blanchot Reader: Fiction & Literary Essays,* trans. Lydia Davis, Paul Auster, and Robert Lamberton (New York: Station Hill Press, 1999), 189–99.—Trans.]

so only by accident and not in an essential or constitutive way. Here we have no knowledge of the law, we do not have a relationship with it based on knowledge,[69] it is neither a subject nor an object *before* which one would have to stand. Nothing holds (up) before the law. The law is not a woman or a female figure, even if the man, *homo* and *vir,* wishes to enter into it or to penetrate it (which is precisely how he is deluded). But neither is the law a man; it is neuter, beyond grammatical or sexual gender, it remains indifferent, impassive, caring little to reply *yes* or *no.* It allows the man to make up his own mind freely, lets him wait, abandons him. And then neuter, neither feminine nor masculine, indifferent because one does not know if it is a (respectable) person or a thing, who or what. The law takes place (without showing itself, and therefore without taking place) in the space of this not-knowing. The guardian watches over this theatre of the invisible, and the man wishes to glimpse it *by stooping down.* Is the law low, lower than him? Or rather, does he bow respectfully before what the narrator of *The Madness of the Day* calls the "knee" of the Law? Unless of course the law is lying down, or, as is said of justice or of its representative, it is "sitting" [*"assise"*]. The law would not remain upright, and this is perhaps another difficulty for whoever might wish to be positioned *before* it. The entire scenography of the narrative is a drama about standing/sitting.[70] At the beginning, at the origin of the story, the gatekeeper and the man are standing, erect, facing each other. At the end of the text, at the interminable but interrupted end of the

---

69. Cf. the chapter "A Politics of Judgment," in Lyotard and Thébaud, *Just Gaming,* 73: "There is no knowledge in matters of ethics. And therefore there will be no knowledge in matters of politics."

70. [This seems to allude to the French *cour d'assisses* (court of assizes) and the *magistrature debout* (state prosecutor). —Trans.]

story, at the end of the man, at the end of his life, the guardian is much taller than his interlocutor. It is then his turn to stoop down, from a height that *overhangs* [*qui surplombe*]; and the story of the law marks the appearance of the preposition *sur*[71] or the difference in height (*Grössenunterschied*). This is progressively modified to the man's detriment. It seems to measure the passing of time in the story. In the interval, that is, in the middle of the text, also the middle of the man's life after he decided to wait, the guardian gives him a stool and sits him down. The man remains there, "sits for days and years," for his whole life. In the end he enters, as we say, a second childhood. The difference of height can also signify the relationship between generations. The child dies old like a little child (on four, two, and then three legs—and don't forget the stool) before a guardian who gets bigger, who is standing and supervising [*sur-veillant*].[72]

The law says nothing, and we are told nothing about it. Nothing, only its name, the common noun, and nothing else. In German it is written with a capital letter, like a proper noun. We do not know what it is, who it is, where it is. Is it a thing, a person, a speech, a voice, a text or simply a nothing that always defers access to itself, interdicting *itself* in this way in order to become something or someone?

In the end the old child almost becomes blind, but he hardly knows it, "he does not know whether the world is really darker or whether his eyes are only deceiving him. Yet in his darkness he is now aware of a radiance that streams inextinguishably from the gateway of the Law."[73] This is the most religious moment of the writing.

---

71. [See note 50 above.—Trans.]

72. [See note 50 above.—Trans.]

73. [The French translation of *Vor dem Gesetz* on which Derrida relies here does not capitalize "law," different from what happens in the English translation.—Trans.]

An analogy with Judaic law: Hegel recounts and interprets in his own way the experience of Pompey. Curious as to what lay behind the doors of the Tabernacle enclosing the Holy of Holies, the Consul approaches the innermost part of the Temple, the center (*Mittelpunkt*) of adoration. Hegel[74] says that he was hoping to find there "a being, an essence offered for his meditation, something that was full of meaning (*Sinnvolles*)[75] being provided for his respect; and when he believed he was entering into this secret (*Geheimnis*), before the ultimate spectacle, he felt mystified, disappointed, deceived (*getäuscht*).[76] He found what he sought in 'an empty room [*einem leeren Raume*],' and he concluded from this that the proper secret was itself through and through foreign, through and through outside of them, the Jews, beyond sight and beyond feeling (*ungesehen und ungefühlt*)." "The transcendence is empty," says Lyotard.[77]

This *différantial* topic postpones, guardian after guardian, in the polarity of the high and the low, of the distant and the close (*fort/da*), of the now and the later. The same topic, having no place of its own, the same atopic, the same madness defers the law like the nothing that interdicts itself and like the neuter that annuls all opposition.

---

74. [Although quotation marks are used in the French, Derrida appears for the most part to be paraphrasing Friedrich Hegel, *On Christianity: Early Theological Writings,* trans. T.M. Knox and Richard Kroner (New York: Harper & Brothers, 1961), 192–3 (Georg Wilhelm Friedrich Hegel, *Frühe Schriften,* Werke I, (Frankfurt am Main: Suhrkamp, 1986), 284–5). The translation within double quotation marks in the text above will be a translation of Derrida's text, and the single quotation marks will indicate where Hegel is directly cited by Derrida.—Trans.]

75. [Derrida's text does not capitalize *Sinnvolles.*—Trans.]

76. [Derrida's text does not have an umlaut on the "a" of *getäuscht.*—Trans.]

77. Lyotard, *Just Gaming,* 69.

The atopic annuls what takes place, the event itself. This act of annulment gives birth to the law, before as before and before as after. That is why there is and there is not place for a narrative. The *différantial* atopic pushes the repetition of the narrative *before the law*. It also confers upon the narrative exactly what it withholds from it, its narrative title. This is as true for the text signed by Kafka bearing the title "Before the Law" as it is for that passage in *The Trial* that seems to tell roughly the same story, a part [*pièce*] that comprises the whole of *The Trial* in the scene of "Before the Law."

It would be tempting, beyond the limits of this reading, to reconstitute this narrative without narrative within, for example, the elliptical framework of the *Critique of Practical Reason* or *Totem and Taboo*. But however far we might pursue such an interpretation, it would not be possible to explain the parable of a narrative termed "literature" with the help of semantic ideas that are philosophical or psychoanalytical in origin, by drawing on some knowledge [*quelque savoir*]. We have seen the necessity of this: The fiction of this ultimate narrative that robs us of any event, this pure narrative or narrative without narrative is as much traversed by philosophy, science, or psychoanalysis as it is by the aforementioned literature.

I conclude. These are the guardian's last words: "I am now going to shut it," I close the gate, I conclude ("Ich gehe jetzt und schliesse ihn").

In a certain medical code the expression *ante portas* refers to the place of premature ejaculation of which Freud claimed to have drawn up the clinical picture, the etiology and the symptomatology. In the text or before the text entitled "Vor dem Gesetz" (*vor,* the preposition *first of all* inscribed in the assigned title "Before the Law"), what happens or does not happen, its place and its nonplace *ante portas,* is this not precisely the nuptial bond [*l'hymen*] with the law, a penetration (*Eintritt*) into the law?

60

The postponement until the death of the old child, of the infant old man, can with equal validity be interpreted as nonpenetration by premature ejaculation or by nonejaculation. The result is the same, the judgment, the conclusion. The tabernacle remains empty and dissemination inevitable [*fatale*]. The relationship with the law remains interrupted, without-relation [*sans-rapport*], which we should not rush to interpret according to the sexual or genital paradigm of *coitus interruptus* or non-coitus [*nul*], of impotence or the neuroses that Freud deciphers here. Might it not be the place [*N'y a-t-il pas lieu*][78] to examine what we calmly call the sexual relationship on the basis of the narrative without narrative of the law? It is very likely that those pleasures that we call normal would not escape this examination.

Might it not be the place [*N'y a-t-il pas lieu*] to examine, I said, using a French idiom that is almost untranslatable. The phrase implies: "we must" examine. The French idiom that lays down the law here also expresses a law: "might it not" means "we must," "it is prescribed, appropriate or necessary to . . .". It is ordered by a law.

And is that not, in effect, what the guardian says? Does he not mean: "there is place for you, here, . . . [*il y a lieu pour toi, ici, . . .*]" There is place for you? We do not know what for, but there is place [*il y a lieu*]. The guardian is not *ante portas* but *ante portam*. He prohibits nothing; he is not guarding the gates but the gate. And he insists on the singularity of this particular gate. The law is neither multiplicity nor, as is believed, universal generality. It is always an idiom, and in that lies the sophistication of Kantianism. Its gate concerns only you, there is only one and it is singularly destined and determined ("nur für dich

---

78. [A less literal interpretation would be "Might it not be appropriate." We however opt here for "place" because of the importance of the notion of place in this context.—Trans.]

bestimmt") for you. At the moment when the man arrives at his end—he is soon going to die—the guardian makes it clear to him that he is not reaching his destination or that his destination is not reaching him [*qu'il n'arrive pas à destination ou que sa destination n'arrive pas à lui*].[79] The man arrives at his end without reaching [*parvenir*] his end. The gateway is destined for him alone and awaits only him, he arrives there but does not arrive at entering there, he does not arrive at arriving there. Such is the narrative of an event that happens *not* to happen [*qui arrive à ne pas arrive*]. The guardian recognizes that the man is already arriving at his end and, because of his diminishing sense of hearing, he roars: "No one else could ever be admitted here, since this gate was made only for you. I am now going to shut it."

Now this is the last word, the conclusion or the closure of the narrative.

The text can be seen as the gateway, the entrance (*Eingang*), which the guardian has just closed. And, as I conclude, I will begin with this sentence (ruling or judgment), with this conclusion formulated by the guardian. When he closes the thing, he will have closed the text. Which nevertheless closes on nothing. The narrative "Before the Law" could be said to recount nothing or to describe nothing but itself as a text. It could be said to be doing only this or doing also this. Not in a confident specular reflection of some auto-referential transparency, and I insist on this point, but in the unreadability of the text, if we want to understand by that the impossibility in which we too find ourselves of being able to have access to its proper sense, to the possibly inconsistent content that it keeps jealously in reserve. The text guards itself, like the law. It speaks only of itself, but then only of its nonidentity with itself. It does not arrive or allow itself to be arrived at [*Il n'arrive ni ne*

---

79. [See note 63 above.—Trans.]

62

laisse arriver à lui-même]. It is the law; it makes the law and leaves the reader before the law.

Let us be precise. We are *before* this text that, saying nothing clear, presenting no identifiable content beyond the narrative itself, except an unending *différance* until death, remains nevertheless rigorously intangible. Intangible: by that I mean inaccessible to contact, impregnable and ultimately ungraspable, incomprehensible, but also that which we do not have the *right* to touch. It is, as we say, an "original" text: it is forbidden or illegitimate to transform or deform it, to tamper with its form. In spite of its nonidentity with itself in its meaning or its direction, in spite of its essential illegibility, its "form" presents and performs itself as a sort of personal identity that has a right to absolute respect. If someone changed a word or altered a sentence in it, a judge could always say that transgression, violence, infidelity had taken place. A bad translation will always be called to appear before the version labeled original, which, we say, *is authoritative,* because it is authorized by the author or those who act on his authority, its identity designated by its title, which is its official name in the registers of the state, framed by its first word and its last. Anyone undermining the original identity of this text might be called to appear before the law. That can happen to any reader in the presence of the text, to the critic, the publisher, the translator, the heirs, teachers. They are all then both guardians and men from the country. On both sides of the divide.

I said the title and the first words: they are, precisely, "Before the Law" and, once more, "Before the law."[80] The final words are: "I am closing [*Je clos*]."[81] The "I" of the guardian is also the "I" of the text or the law; it announces the

---

80. [See note 73 above. The same applies here.—Trans.]

81. [The French *clore* also means "to bring to a conclusion."—Trans.]

identity with itself of a corpus that has been bequeathed, of an inheritance that expresses nonidentity with itself. Neither of these is natural, but is rather the result of a legal performative. This (and this is undoubtedly what is referred to as writing, the action and the signature of the "writer")[82] *poses before* us, preposes[83] or proposes a text that lays down the law, and in the first place concerning itself. In its very act it states and produces the law that protects it and makes it inviolable [*intangible*]. It does and it states, it states what it does by doing what it states. This possibility is implicit in every text, even when it does not have the evidently auto-referential form of this one. At the same time both allegorical and tautological, Kafka's narrative works across the referentially naïve unfolding of its narration, which goes through a gateway that it encompasses [*une porte qu'elle comporte*], an internal limit that opens on to nothing, before nothing, on to the ob-ject of no possible experience.

"Before the Law," the title says. "Vor dem Gesetz," the title says.

"Before the Law" says the title. "Vor dem Gesetz" says the title.

The text bears its title and bears on its title. Would its proper object, if it had one, not be the effect produced by the play in the title? To demonstrate and develop in an ellipsis the powerful operation of the given title?

You have not forgotten my question: how to judge Jean-François Lyotard? Who is Jean-François Lyotard? I do

---

82. [There is no closing parenthesis in the French.—Trans.]

83. [Dictionaries in general translate the French *préposer* as "to appoint"; "to place" or "to put somebody in charge of." To retain the wordplay in the French, we render it here as "prepose," a now-obsolete word, which originally derives from the French *préposer* and which inter alia meant "to set over," "to appoint as chief or superior," "to propose," "to intend" (*Oxford English Dictionary*, 2nd ed. (Oxford: Clarendon Press, 1989)).—Trans.]

not know if these questions can be completely separated from topology: in which location does Jean-François Lyotard take place? The guardian's location? The man from the country's location? The law's location? Unless perhaps, here, it is the location of the title and the signature, which *is* the title or which *gives* the title. All of these locations at the same time, all of these locations in succession?

One begins to dream, and to wish it were possible to join the idiomatic and the categorical together, end to end. And then, why should there not be another location, an additional location, outside the program and the situations that I have just named? There is the dream, and there is the awakening. It is not reality that awakens, but what (in opposition to the fantasy, as its very possibility, the impassive severity of its law) I prefer to call Necessity. For this there is no other location. But, inversely, it has no meaning—either idiomatic or categorical—without the dream, and without the fantasy either. And that is the tragedy, the destinerring [*destinerrance*][84] of destiny.

The gateway also separates the title from itself. Or rather it interposes itself between the expression "Before the Law" understood as title or proper name and the *same* expression as *incipit*. It divides the origin. As we have said, the *incipit* is part of the narrative, and does not have the same value or the same referent as the title; but, as *incipit,* its place in the body of the text is singular. It marks the boundary that guarantees the identity of the corpus. Between the two events of "Before the Law," within the repetition itself, a line passes that separates two borders. It splits the border by dividing the nature of the expression [*Elle dédouble la limite en divisant le trait*]. But

---

84. [We adopt here the translation by Catherine Porter and Philip Lewis of "destinerrance" in "No Apocalypse, Not Now," in Derrida, *Psyche I*, 404–5. —Trans.]

the homonymy remains impassive, as if nothing had happened. It is as if nothing had come to pass.

I conclude. I interrupt here this type of analysis that, in its details, could be pursued very far, and I come back to my initial question.

What would allow us to judge that this text belongs to "literature"? And, following from that, what is literature? I am afraid that this question remains unanswered. Does it not betray, once again, the rustic naivety of a man from the country? But that would not be enough to disqualify it, and the man's reason imperturbably reasserts its right; it is untiring at any age.

If we subtract from this text all those elements that could belong to another register (day-to-day information, history, erudition, philosophy, fiction, etc., in brief, anything that is not necessarily associated with literature), we have an obscure sense that what is *operative* and *at work* [*fait œuvre*] in this text retains [*garde*] an essential relation with the play of framing and the paradoxical logic of boundaries, which somehow perturbs the "normal" system of reference, while at the same time *revealing* an essential structure of referentiality. Obscure revelation of referenti-ali*ty* that no longer makes reference, does not refer, just as the eventuali*ty* of the event is no longer an event.

But the fact that it is at work [*fasse œuvre*] nevertheless does perhaps gesture in the direction of literature. It is perhaps an insufficient gesture, but a necessary one: there can be no literature without a work, without some absolutely singular performance, and this necessary irreplace-ability calls forth once more the questions posed by the man from the country when the singular intersects with the universal, when the categorical implicates the idiomatic, as any literature must always do. The man from the country had trouble understanding the singularity of an entry that had to be universal, as it was in fact. He had trouble with literature.

How can we verify the subtraction about which I spoke a moment ago? Well, there is a crosscheck suggested by *The Trial* itself. We find there the same *content* in a different framework, with another system of boundaries and above all without a proper title, with no other title than that of a volume containing a few hundred pages. The same content, from a literary point of view, gives rise to a completely different work. What is different, from one work to the other, is neither the *content* nor the *form* (the signifying expression, the phenomena of language and rhetoric). It is the movements of framing and referentiality.

These two works, therefore, along the line of their strange filiation, become metonymic interpretations of each other, each one becoming the absolutely independent part of the other, a part that becomes progressively larger than the whole. The title of the other. That is still not enough. If the framework, the title and the referential structure are necessary for the creation of the literary work as such, these conditions of possibility are still too general and apply to other texts to which[85] we would not think of attaching any literary value. These possibilities grant a text the authority to *dictate the law*, beginning with its own. But on condition that the text itself must appear *before the law* of another text, another more powerful text, guarded by more powerful guardians. In effect, the text (for example, what we call a "literary" text, particularly this narrative by Kafka) before which we, the readers, appear as before the law, this text, guarded by its guardians (author, publisher, critics, academics, archivists, librarians, lawyers, etc.) can legislate only if a system of more powerful

---

85. [A spelling mistake appears here in the French text. The first word of page 132 should be *auxquels*. —Trans.]

laws ("a more powerful doorkeeper") guarantees it, beginning with the ensemble of laws or social conventions that authorize all these legitimacies.

If Kafka's text says all that about literature, the powerful ellipsis it offers us does not belong entirely to literature. The place from which it speaks to us *about* the laws of literature, about the law without which no literary specificity could take shape or have consistency, that place cannot be simply *within* literature.

There are most probably grounds for elaborating *together* a certain historicity of law and a certain historicity of literature. If I say "literature" rather than poetry or belles-lettres, I do so in order to indicate that hypothesis according to which the relatively modern specificity of literature as such retains a close and essential relationship with a moment in the history of law. In another culture, or in Europe at another moment in the history of positive law, of (explicit or implicit) legislation on the ownership of written works, for example during the Middle Ages or before the Middle Ages, the identity of this text, its play with the title, with signatures, with its borders or those of other corpuses, this entire framing system would function differently and with other conventional guarantees. This is not to say that in the Middle Ages it would not have counted on institutional protection and oversight.[86] But this regulated the identity of corpuses in an entirely different way,

---

86. Cf. Dragonetti, *Le conte du Graal,* 52ff. in particular. I also refer to the works of Ernst Kantorowicz, in particular to one of his articles recently published in France, "La souveraineté de l'artiste, Note sur les maximes juridiques et les théories esthétiques de la Renaissance," *Poésie* 18 (1981): 3–21, translated from English ["The Sovereignty of the Artist: A Note on Legal Maxims and Renaissance Theories of Art," in *De Artibus Opuscula XL: Essays in Honor of Erwin Panofsky* (New York 1961), 267–79—Trans.] by JF Courtine Courtine and S-Denamy. This article was republished in Ernst Hartwig Kantorowicz, *Selected Studies* (New York: J.J. Augustin, 1965).

and handed them over much more easily to the transfor-
mative initiative of copyists or other "guardians," to the
grafts added on by heirs or other "authors" (anonymous
or not, masked or not by individual or collective pseudo-
nyms that can, to a greater or lesser extent, be identified).
But, whatever the structure of the legal and therefore political institution that guarantees the work, this work appears and always remains *before the law*. It has existence
and consistency only on the conditions imposed by law
and it becomes "literature" only in an age [*époque*] when
law regulates the problems of the ownership of creative
works, the identity of corpuses, the value of signatures, the
difference between creating, producing, and reproducing,
etc. In broad terms, this law became established between
the end of the seventeenth century and the beginning of
the nineteenth century in Europe. It remains the case that
the concept of literature that underpins the law relating
to creative works remains obscure. The positive laws to
which I refer are also valid for other arts and they shed
no critical light on their own conceptual presuppositions. What concerns me here is that these obscure presuppositions have also been inherited by the "guardians,"
critics, academics, theoreticians of literature, writers, phi-
losophers. They must all appeal to a law, appear before it,
watch over it and at the same time allow themselves to be
monitored by it. All of them naively interrogate its singularity and its universality, and none of them receives a reply
that does anything other than reaffirm *différance*: there is
(no) more law and (no) more literature [*plus de loi et plus
de littérature*].

In this sense Kafka's text perhaps also enunciates the
being-before-the-law of all texts. The text enunciates this
elliptically, advancing it and withdrawing it at the same
time. It does not belong solely to the literature of a particular age [*époque*] because the text itself stands before the
law (which it enunciates), before a certain type of law. It

also points obliquely to literature, it speaks of itself as a literary effect. And in so doing it goes beyond the literature about which it speaks.

But is there not a case for saying that all literature goes beyond literature? What would literature be if it were only what it is, literature? It would no longer be itself if it were itself. That is also part of the ellipsis of "Before the Law." It is certainly not possible to speak of "literariness" [*littérarité*] as a *belonging* to Literature [*la littérature*], as the inclusion of a phenomenon or an object, even a creative work, within a field [*dans un champ*], a domain, a region whose boundaries are pure and whose titles are indivisible. The work, the opus, does not belong to the field [*champ*]; it is the transformer of the field [*il est transformateur du champ*].[87]

Literature has perhaps come to occupy, in historical conditions that are not simply linguistic, a place that is always open to a sort of subversive juridicity [*juridicité*]. It may have occupied that place for quite a while without itself being thoroughly subversive, sometimes quite the contrary. This subversive juridicity supposes that identity with self is never assured or reassuring. It also supposes a power to produce performatively statements made by the law, by the law that can be literature and not only the law that subjects literature to itself. It therefore makes the law; it emerges in that place where law is made. But, under certain conditions, it can also make use of the legislative power of linguistic performativity in order to circumvent the existing laws from which it nevertheless obtains the safeguards and the conditions of its emergence. And it does so thanks to the referential ambiguity of certain linguistic structures. Under those conditions, literature can *trick the law* [*jouer la loi*], repeat it while also deflecting

---

87. [See the discussion above by Derrida of *Duchamp's TRANS/ formers.*—Trans.]

it or going around it. Those conditions, which are also the conventional conditions of any performative, are undoubtedly not purely linguistic, although any convention can in its turn give rise to a definition or a contract that is rooted in language. We touch here on one of those points that are the most difficult to situate when we must rediscover [*retrouver*] language without language, language beyond language, these force relations, mute but already haunted by writing, in which the conditions of the performative, the rules of the game [*les règles du jeu*], and the limits of subversion are established.

In that ungraspable moment when it tricks the law [*joue la loi*], literature goes beyond literature. It finds itself on both sides of the line that separates the law from the outside-the-law [*hors-la-loi*]; it divides the being-before-the-law, it is at one and the same time, like the man from the country, "before the law" and "ahead of the law" [*"devant la loi" et "avant la loi"*]. Ahead of the being-before-the-law, which is also that of the guardian. But in such an improbable location, will it have taken place [*aura-t-elle eu lieu*]? And, will it have been the place [*Et y aura-t-il eu lieu*] to speak of literature?

This has been the scene for a reading that was only minimally categorical. I have risked glosses, have given multiple interpretations, asked and avoided answering questions, abandoned decoding before it was complete, and left enigmas intact, beginning with Jean-François Lyotard, I have accused, acquitted, defended, praised, and summoned to appear. The scene for this reading seemed to be bustling around a narrative in isolation. But apart from the metonymic hand-to-hand exchanges that might be possible with *Zur Frage der Gesetze* or chapter 7 of Paul's Epistle to the Romans, this exegetical dramatization is perhaps only, and above all, a part or a moment, a fragment of *The Trial*. In that case everything you have just heard has become, in advance, a *mise-en-abyme,* everything except Jean-François Lyotard or everything that has to do here with his name. Here you have, perhaps, a possible reply, even if it appears to you to fall under negative predication, as one says in negative theology: Jean-François Lyotard is—or we will say, here, today, that he is—all that which cannot be metonymized *en abyme* by the Talmudic scene into which I have perhaps plunged with you. For if *The Trial* places, in advance, everything you have just heard into a *mise-en-abyme,* it is possible that "Before the Law" does the same by means of a yet more powerful ellipsis into which *The Trial* plunges, taking us along with it. Chronology has very little importance here, even if, as we know, Kafka published only "Before the Law," under this title, during his lifetime. The structural possibility of this counter-*abyme* is open to challenge from this chronological order.

In *The Trial* (chapter IX, "In the Cathedral"),[88] the text that constitutes the totality of "Before the Law," with the exception, naturally, of the title, is reported *in inverted commas* by a priest.[89] This priest is not simply a narrator; he is someone who quotes or re-tells a narration. He cites a narrative that does not belong to the text of the law in the Scriptures, but, he says, "to the writings which preface the Law" ["den einleitenden Schriften zum Gesetz"]: "You're deluding yourself about the Court", the priest said [to K.]. "In the writings which preface the Law it says about this delusion: before the Law stands a door-keeper,"

88. [Franz Kafka, *The Trial,* trans. Douglas Scott and Chris Walker (London and Basingstoke: Picador, 1977). Subsequent page citations are in the text.—Trans.]

89. [See Heinz Politzer, *Franz Kafka: Paradox and Parable* (Ithaca, N.Y., Cornell University Press, 1962), 176, who points out that Kafka saw in himself both something of his father (a boorish man from the country), and his mother (who descended from the priestly Levites).—Trans.]

etc. (239). The whole chapter is an astonishing Talmudic exegesis, on the subject of "Before the Law," between the priest and K. We would need hours to study its texture, to pick it apart and grapple with its meaning.[90] The general law of this scene is that the text (the short narrative in inverted commas, "Before the Law," if you like), which seems to be the object of the hermeneutic dialogue between the priest and K., is also the program, down to the minutest detail, of the exegetical altercation to which it gives rise, the priest and K. being, by turns, the guardian and the man from the country, exchanging places before the law, mimicking each other, each putting himself ahead of the other. Not a single detail is missing, and we could, if you wish, demonstrate this in another session of patient reading. I do not want to keep you here right to the end of the day, or to the end of your days, even though you are seated, and seated not at the door, but within the castle itself.[91] To finish, I will simply quote a few passages from the chapter, rather like white pebbles set down along a pathway or on the tomb of Rabbi Loew, which I saw in Prague a few months ago, on the eve of an arrest and an investigation without trial, during which the representatives of the law asked me, among other things, if the philosopher I was going to visit was a "Kafkologue" (I had said that I had *also* come to Prague to follow the trail of Kafka); my own lawyer, appointed as my legal representative, had said to me: "It must feel as though you are living out a story by Kafka"; and as he left me: "Don't take it too tragically, live it as a literary experience." And when I said that I had

90. [The French reads: "en étudier le grain, les poux et les puces": literally: "the grain, the lice and the fleas." The expression "chercher des poux" means "to nitpick"; and "cela m'a mis la puce à l'oreille" means "to start one thinking." —Trans.]

91. [An allusion to the castle of Cerisy-la-Salle, where Derrida presented the present paper. —Trans.]

never previously seen the drugs that the customs officers claimed to have found in my bag, the prosecutor replied: "That's what all drug traffickers say."

Here then are the little white pebbles. The subject is prejudgment and prejudice:

> "But I am not guilty," said K. "It's a mistake. How can a person be guilty at all? Surely we are all human beings here, one like the other."
>
> "That's right," said the priest, "but that is the way the guilty are wont to talk."
>
> "Are you prejudiced against me?" K. asked.
>
> "No, I'm not prejudiced against you," said the priest.
>
> "I'm grateful to you," K. said. "But everybody else who is concerned in these proceedings is prejudiced against me. They make even those who aren't involved prejudiced against me. My position is getting more difficult all the time."
>
> "You are failing to understand the facts of the case," the priest said. "The verdict does not come all at once, the proceedings gradually merge into the verdict." (236)

After the priest had told K. the untitled story—of "before the law" taken from the writings that *preface* the law—[92] K.'s conclusion was that "the door-keeper deceived the man" (240). At which point the priest—identifying himself somewhat with the guardian—undertakes the defense of the guardian in the course of a lengthy reading in Talmudic style beginning with the words "You don't show enough respect for what is written, and you're changing the

---

92. [The French text has a comma here, though a dash appears to be required.—Trans.]

story . . .". During the course of this reading, among other things that serve particularly well for reading the very unreadability of "Before the Law," he warns: "Commentators say: 'The correct interpretation of a certain subject and misunderstanding of the same subject do not wholly exclude each other'" (242).

The second stage: he convinces K., who then identifies with the guardian and agrees with him. The priest immediately overturns the interpretation and changes their identificatory places:

> "You know the story in more detail than I do, and you've known it longer," K. said.
>
> They were both silent for a while. Then K. said:
>
> "So you don't believe the man was deceived?"
>
> "Don't misunderstand me," the priest said, "I'm only telling you the different opinions there are about it. You mustn't pay too much attention to them. The scripture is unalterable, and the opinions are often merely an expression of despair on the part of the commentators. In this case one opinion even has it that it is the door-keeper himself who is deceived."
>
> "That's going a bit far, isn't it?" K. said. "What's the evidence for that?" (243)

There then follows a second exegetico-Talmudic movement on the part of the priest, who is both a cleric [*abbé*] and a rabbi, to some extent a sort of Saint Paul, the Paul of

93. [Romans 7:6, *NRSV.* Derrida's quotation "dont la lettre a vieilli" is taken from the Louis Segond French Bible, Romans 7, verse 6: "non selon la lettre qui a vieilli." The English version that comes closest to this sense is the *NRSV,* quoted here; most earlier English versions, including the King James, give "the oldness of the letter," which does not closely correspond to Derrida's text. —Trans.]

the Epistle to the Romans who speaks according to the law, about the law, and against the law, "the old written code";[93] the Saint Paul who also says that "if it had not been for the law, I would not have known sin":"I was once alive apart from the law, but when the commandment came, sin revived and I died."[94]

"'The evidence for that,' answered the cleric, 'is based on the premise of the door-keeper's simple-mindedness. It's argued that he doesn't know the inner world of the Law. He only knows the path to it, and the entrance to that path which he has constantly to patrol. The ideas he has of that inner world are felt to be childish, and it's thought that he himself fears what he tries to make the man afraid of. Yes, he fears it even more than the man . . .'" (243).

I leave you to read the rest of this ineffable scene, in which the priest-rabbi endlessly picks apart [d'épouiller]—or grapples with [d'épuceler]—this narrative, in an attempt to explain the minutest detail [cherche jusqu'à la petite bête].[95]

Everything in this passage subsumes [comprend] "Before the Law," but without subsuming it, into a *mise-en-abyme*, for example the glow that has something of the tabernacle about it ("The torch he was holding had long since gone out. Once the silver statue of a saint shone directly in front of him, but only with the gleam of its own silver, and then immediately vanished into the darkness [Saint Paul, perhaps]. In order not to be completely dependent on the priest, K. asked him: 'Aren't we near the main entrance now?' 'No,' said the priest, 'we're a long way away. Do you want to go now?'" (247), or again, in the same counter-*abyme* of "Before the Law" it is K. who asks the cleric to

---

94. [See Romans 7: 7, 9–10, *NRSV.*—Trans.]

95. [The French expression *chercher la petite bête* means "to split hairs." See further note 90 above.—Trans.]

wait and this same request goes so far as to ask the priest-interpreter to do the asking himself. It is K. who asks him to ask. ("'Wait, please, just a moment!' 'I'm waiting,' said the priest. 'Don't you want anything more from me?' K. asked. 'No,' said the priest." [247]). We should not forget that the cleric, just like the guardian in the story, is a representative of the law, also a guardian, because he is the prison chaplain. And he reminds K. not that he is himself the guardian or the prison chaplain, but that K. must first understand and himself announce who the priest is. These are the last words of the chapter:

"'But you must first understand who I am,' said the priest.

'You're the prison chaplain,' K. said, moving closer to the priest. His immediate return to the bank was not as necessary as he had made out, he could perfectly well stay here a little longer.

'Therefore I belong to the Court,' the priest said. 'So why should I want anything from you? *Das Gericht will nichts von dir. Es nimmt dich auf, wenn du kommst, und es entläßt dich, wenn du gehst.* The Court doesn't want anything from you. It receives you when you come, and it dismisses you when you go'" (248).

P.S. I am grateful to Denis Kambouchner who, a few months after this conference, drew my attention to this passage in *Conversations with Kafka,* by Gustav Janouch.[96] Kafka is speaking:

"... I am no critic. I am only a man under judgment and a spectator."

"And the judge?" I [i.e., Janouch] asked.

96. [Gustav Janouch, *Conversations with Kafka,* 2nd ed., trans. Goronway Rees (New York: New Directions, 2012), 14.—Trans.]

He gave an embarrassed smile. "Indeed, I am also the usher of the court, yet I do not know the judges. Probably I am quite a humble assistant-usher. I have no definite [*définitif*] post." Kafka laughed. I laughed with him, though I did not understand him.

"The only definite [*définitif*] thing is suffering," he said earnestly. "When do you write?"

Why definitive [*définitif*]? Doubtless in order also to say both "decisive" and "determinant," *entscheidend* (the word does have both senses, and it is undoubtedly judgment that is being referred to, since it is always both critical and final).

Jacques Derrida (1930–2004) was director of studies at the École des hautes études en sciences sociales, Paris, and professor of humanities at the University of California, Irvine. The unpublished seminars of Derrida, of which there are twenty volumes and which stretch over a period of more than forty years, are currently in the process of being published.

Sandra van Reenen is lecturer in French at the University of the Western Cape, South Africa.

Jacques de Ville is professor of law at the University of the Western Cape, South Africa. His recent publications include *Jacques Derrida: Law as Absolute Hospitality* and *Constitutional Theory: Schmitt after Derrida*.